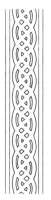

LANGUAGE, SIGN, AND GENDER IN *BEOWULF*

Gillian R. Overing

SOUTHERN ILLINOIS UNIVERSITY PRESS
Carbondale and Edwardsville

Edited by William Jerman
Designed by Liz Fett
Production supervised by Natalia Nadraga

Library of Congress Cataloging-in-Publication Data

Overing, Gillian R., 1952–
    Language, sign, and gender in Beowulf / Gillian R. Overing.
        p.   cm.
    Bibliography: p.
    Includes index.
    1. Beowulf.   2. Semiotics and literature.   3. Feminism and
literature.   4. English poetry—Old English, ca. 450–1100—History
and criticism—Theory, etc.   I. Title.
    PR1585.O94   1989
    829'.3—dc19   89–5922
    ISBN 0–8093–1563–7   CIP

The paper used in this publication meets the minimum requirements of
American National Standard for Information Sciences —Permanence of
Paper for Printed Library Materials, ANSI Z39.48-1984. ∞

for Steve

Contents

Acknowledgments

I should like to thank Wake Forest University, especially Provost Edwin Wilson and Dean Thomas Mullen, for supporting my work in the practical form of release time and research leave. I thank friends and colleagues who were always willing to listen and who helped me work through ideas at different stages: Sally Barbour, Mary DeShazer, Teri Marsh, Helen Warren, and Kari Weil. I thank also my colleagues Nancy Cotton, Robert Hedin, Dolly McPherson, and Elizabeth Phillips, who have offered me their knowledge, friendship, and encouragement. I owe a special debt of gratitude to Allen Frantzen and James Hans for reading and commenting on my work, and giving me invaluable support both as critics and friends. I should also like to express my gratitude to Michael Shapiro, who directed an NEH summer seminar in Princeton in 1984 and introduced me to the work of Charles S. Peirce, and who has been a regular reader and loyal supporter of my work ever since.

Parts of chapters 1 and 2 have appeared in print before, in *Concerning Poetry* vol. 19 (1986), and in the *American Journal of Semiotics* 5:1 (1987), and I am grateful for permission to reprint them here in altered form.

Finally, I want to thank my husband Steve Ford for his patient and unquestioning support. The completion of this manuscript is a testimony to the steadiness and generosity of his spirit.

Introduction

> The kind of bringing-together proposed here has the structure
> of an interlacing, a weaving, or a web, which would allow the
> different threads and different lines of sense or force to
> separate again, as well as being ready to bind others together.
> —Jacques Derrida, *Speech and Phenomena*

When I first began to study Old English poetry, I found
it difficult to connect this kind of poetry with any other. It opened
up a strange new territory, novel and intriguing despite (or
perhaps because of) its formality, curious and somehow bizarre
despite the hours of mundane paradigm and vocabulary learning
that it rigorously demanded. I was inclined to agree with Thomas
Shippey who claims that this poetry is different "*in kind*" from
other types, although my sense of just *how* it was different in kind
was articulated most often by default. The problem was, and is,
that Old English poetry finds no space to occupy within the
confines of accepted, agreed upon, or already delineated, literary
borders. Its rhythms and sounds, its form and content do not
respond to ready-made interpretive strategies; it does not "keep
the bargain of modern poetry—that nothing vital will be left out
and nothing unnecessary put in" (Shippey, 13). It demands in-
stead a renegotiation of any such bargain, a made-to-order inter-
pretive strategy, or variety of strategies, that embrace and revalue
its difference.

While I still retain a strong sense of the uniqueness of Old
English poetry, and a fascination for its powerful peculiarities, the
nature of its apparent separateness—the idea of its difference—
has become increasingly aligned and identified with theoretical
attempts to examine notions of difference in organic, creative,
and nonreductive ways. Generally speaking, it remains true that
Anglo-Saxonists have been circumspect about admitting or wel-
coming theoretical insights, preferring the more "solid ground"
of the historical and philological.

Theory of various kinds has been met with varying degrees of suspicion. If we take a brief look at some responses to linguistic theory, for example, we can see this scholarly circumspection and suspicion clearly expressed. (I choose linguistic theory because it is arguably the most influential precursor of other forms of theoretical approaches, deconstructionist, semiotic, psychoanalytic, feminist, and so forth.) At one extreme, Bruce Mitchell rejects outright the value of linguistic theory. In an analysis of literary and linguistic factors aimed at delimiting the scope of differing opinions in certain textual instances, he insists that he is employing "not linguistic *arguments,* but linguistic *facts*" (11), and that his use of linguistics "has no reference to its present day use by practitioners of a 'science' which has hijacked the word and which in many of its aspects will (I believe) prove to be one of the great non-subjects of the twentieth century" (11n).

Less condemnatory, but nonetheless circumspect, is Stanley Greenfield's response. In the introduction to *The Interpretation of Old English Poems,* entitled "Towards a Critical Framework," Greenfield acknowledges the benefits of variety and openness in critical approaches, but remains suspicious of the separate validity of linguistic insights; commenting on the work of Roman Jakobson, he writes: "I suspect that the valuable critical perceptions do not really emerge from the results of systematic application of linguistic description but are coincident with it, because he is a true-born critic as well as linguist" (28).

From these two examples we might conclude that the reception of linguistic theory has been lukewarm at best, but this situation is gradually changing. In "Linguistics, Literary Criticism, and Old English," Matthew Marino attempts to allay some of this suspicion of theory, addressing critical reservations—those of Mitchell and Greenfield in particular—about the value of linguistic theory for Old English scholarship. He demonstrates some of its clarifying and illuminating possibilities, and looks forward to the expansion of outlook offered by a "level of theory which can translate insight and techniques from one discipline to the other" (11). Some scholars have begun just such a cross-disciplinary expansion, and I mention here but a few examples. Allen J. Frantzen and Charles L. Venegoni in "The Desire for Origins: An Archaeological Analysis of Anglo-Saxon Studies" deconstruct the political, ideological, and cultural assumptions implicit in the history of Anglo-Saxon scholarship. Martin Irvine examines the principles of semiosis and intertextuality in poetry in an attempt to define "the larger signifying systems of Anglo-Saxon culture" (175). Jonathan Evans finds some specific applications for semiotic theory in "Irony and Ambiguity in the Medieval Dragon Code."[1] There have also been some recent discussions of *Beowulf* and other Old English poems that make use of theory, ranging from deconstructionist to psychoanalytic to feminist, which I shall refer to in the following chapters.

I am aware that in addition to the problem of external imposition, there is some margin for error, some presumption, some risk of inappropriateness of several kinds in examining a thousand-year-old body of poetry from more recent theoretical perspectives. The prospect becomes more exciting and potentially productive, however, when theory meshes with practice in an isomorphic relation of mutual reciprocity — when one continually suggests and generates the other. *Beowulf,* for example, offers an ideal model of an already deconstructed, even a continually self-deconstructing, text. What Edward W. Said says of the modern writer's work also holds true for this ancient poem: "the text yields up its formal completeness to a constantly reforged discursivity or productivity" (1975: 176).

Moreover, the "production" of *Beowulf* takes place on several levels, both within and without the text. Frantzen and Venegoni have looked at what, and who, have produced *Beowulf* historically, how meaning has been continually revised by manuscript emendation, how scholars have literally "invented" the text. My primary concern will be the production of meaning within the text (perhaps how this text "invents" us) and the reader's role in this process — a notion that I will explore from several points of view. The internal mode of meaning production in *Beowulf* is nothing if not discursive; or, paraphrasing a frequent student reaction, "this is a very complicated poem and it's hard to keep it all in your mind at the same time." Its arcane structure describes cyclical repetitions and patterned intersections of themes that baffle a linear perspective, and suggest instead the irresolution and dynamism of the deconstructionist free play of textual elements. Similarly, this dynamic aspect of the poem finds resonance and illumination in the insights of semiotic, feminist, and psychoanalytic criticism.

Old English poetry in general, and *Beowulf* in particular, provide a fertile testing ground, or perhaps more aptly, a playing field, for a variety of theoretical preoccupations: the relation of self, or presence, to the text (and here I mean a twentieth-century concept of "self" with all its attendant complexities); the nature and mode of poetic language and of the interpretive process; the location and examination of teleology, of textual boundaries, and of the construction of meaning. While I do not intend to take on the entire Old English canon, I shall be addressing some of these broad critical issues as they are raised in *Beowulf*, as I think the poem itself suggests them. The primary aim of this study will be to address the poem on its own terms, to trace and develop an interpretive strategy consonant with the terms of its difference, and, in the manner of Lévi-Strauss's *bricoleur*, to make use of whatever is at hand: to employ theoretical insights as these seem useful or appropriate. And although my primary focus will be *Beowulf*, I shall also make use of other Old English poems where these seem useful or appropriate.

I run several risks throughout this entire enterprise; theoreticians may require more discussion of theory, and readers interested in *Beowulf* may find the theory inappropriate or at odds with the poem, or may want more specific discussion of the text. In response to these potential dissatisfactions, I invoke the essentially experimental nature of *bricolage* which takes on meaning in difference (Derrida, 1972: 256). The *bricoleur* uses "the instruments which he finds at his disposition around him, those which are already there, which had not been especially conceived with an eye to the operation for which they are to be used and to which one tries by trial and error to adapt them, not hesitating to change them whenever it appears necessary, or to try several of them at once" (Derrida, 1972: 255). The process of *bricolage* can be haphazard, unschematic, and, most important, it is not necessarily "original." I want to stress that I do not aim to produce novel readings of *Beowulf*; many of the comments or insights about the poem might be familiar to readers in another guise or context. I shall be looking at *how*, rather than *what* the poem means, and at ways of describing our interaction with it. I also emphasize that the *bricoleur* aims "not to bring an end to the play of questioning but to extend it" (Hans, 163), and seeks not dominion over, but participation in the process of meaning construction.

The following chapters represent an attempt to match and describe the mode of *Beowulf* in several respects. Insofar as the nature of the poem's complex linguistic and thematic structure mediates against a single encompassing overview and resists the finitude and resolution of interpretive conclusion, I have tried not to follow where the poem does not lead. I do not offer a comprehensive definition of, or explanation for, either the mode or meaning of the poem. In my experience students initially wrestling with the poem want to decide whether Beowulf is right or wrong, whether Hrothgar is weak or strong, whether either is Christian or pagan, whether Wealhtheow is pathetic or dignified, whether Unferth is a fool or a smart coward, whether Grendel and his mother are totally detestable or really quite poignant characters, whether or when they should feel uplifted or devastated by the events of this poem, and so on. Teaching this poem can be in itself a deconstructionist exercise in dismantling hierarchical oppositions; it is often a process of persuading students away from making a choice, and suggesting that they try to achieve instead the balancing act that is the poem, entertaining both or more possibilities in an ongoing process of cross-reference and connection. The result (sometimes a headache!) can be a welcoming receptivity to the poem's complexity, an acceptance of the impossibility, and an understanding of the inappropriateness of coming to any categoric conclusion, any simple summation.

Accordingly, these interrelated discussions of the poem will aim to discover "a strategy without finality" (Derrida, 1973: 135), or rather several strategies: to propose essentially inconclusive but nevertheless regenerative metaphors or analogies where meaning is discovered in process, and as a process of ongoing translation. Running through each of the chapters is one more or less continuous thread, a mode of perception variously imaged by metaphors of weaving—the interwoven fabric of language, the interlace structure of the web of signs, and the weaving of connection, of peace, between peoples, embodied and enacted through women. The metaphor of weaving will recur insistently throughout this text in a variety of forms, but the most fundamental aspects that I want to borrow from it are those of open-ended movement, of ongoing, multifaceted process, of continuity, and the continual possibility of connection.

In Derrida's formulation, the web is a structure that "allows" a multiplicity of comings-together and separations; it facilitates the play of difference and both the separation and convergence of "lines of sense or force"; it evokes an inherent potential for expansion in that these lines stand "*ready* to bind others together" (my italics). I will use this metaphor of weaving not only to talk about the poem but also to talk about how I talk about the poem, allowing interaction, cross-reference, and coincidence on theoretical and textual levels. Ideally, then, one piece of my text will find resonance in another; the chapters will create a "web" of their own. The central concepts of each chapter can be labeled, progressively, as metonymy, interlace, and gender; these function as verbal "strands," the most often used materials, or colors, in this textual web. Each is designed to trace, parallel, or highlight some part of the complex movement that weaves the web of the poem. Each addresses itself to the powerful complexities of *Beowulf*, to describe why it is "so difficult to keep it all in your mind at the same time."

While the chapters might find overall connection in the construct of the web, they differ somewhat in their approach to the question of the relation of language to the subject, the relation of the self, or presence, to the text. In broad summary, chapter 1 posits the self/reader as a function of the text/language, examining the ways in which the text "speaks" the reader. Chapter 2 adopts a more collaborative viewpoint; it develops an interactive semiotic strategy in an attempt to describe an isomorphic relation between poem and reader, between text and self. Chapter 3 addresses the notions of text and self as more complex functions or formulations of desire, and thus complicates and expands the arguments of the two preceding chapters. The final chapter examines the issue of desire in the poem, and, to a lesser extent, desire in the reader (insofar as these may legitimately be viewed as distinct from each other).

The issue of desire in the reader must engage the entire problematic of self—what produces it and how it is produced, what it desires and how it is defined by desire, whether it is unitary, how it is "engendered" within and without the text, indeed what kind of *Beowulf* it wants. These important and fascinating questions will be briefly addressed, but lie for the most part beyond the scope of the present study. Chapter 3 pays more attention to the workings of desire within the narrative, to the ways in which desire is directed, redirected, and conflicted within the poem, when it is viewed through the lens of gender. Although the arrangement of these arguments follows the intersectional patterning of weaving, rather than a linear progressivity, the chapters accrue a progressive complexity; the last chapter's discussion of the problematic of desire and gender in the poem builds on, recasts, and to some extent incorporates the linguistic and semiotic arguments of chapters 1 and 2.

Chapter 1 examines aspects of poetic diction in *Beowulf* and a variety of Old English poems. It has a slightly broader scope in that it does not focus solely on *Beowulf* and aims to create an "overview-in-process," a means of describing the mode of this poetic language as well as accounting for the experience of it—that is, the effect upon the reader. It proposes that the standard characteristics of Old English poetic diction—alliteration, repetition, variation, parataxis, use of formulas, word compounds, "kennings," antithesis, understatement—can be recast as features of the metonymic mode in language. The contiguous, dyadic alignment of metonymic phrases or ideas resists the interpretive closure of metaphor, where meaning is construed, governed, by a third element, a collocating reader or the poet's contextual directive. In terms of the overarching metaphor of weaving, the language of the text weaves its own open-ended, metonymic fabric. From the "kenning" (which I call a metonymic compound), to the paratactic or agrammatical juxtaposition of ideas, to the habit of "digression" on a broader scale, the metonymic mode allows greater flexibility and freedom of association. Unlike metaphor, metonymy does not require mediation or transference of meaning; it does not demand that we see one thing in terms of something else, but rather that we accept and allow the more immediate impact and effect of the poem.

Positing the principle of metonymy as a critical aegis for various facets of Old English poetic diction has several advantages: it offers another means of reexamining critical and stylistic issues; it can create a context for the readers' response, and it can also provide an opportunity to examine the process of meaning construction in Old English poetry and the nature of our interpretive activity. For example, such an approach engages questions of coincidence or coexistence in the Anglo-Saxon period from a linguistic vantage point, in terms of a metonymic self-referential "pagan" vision and a metaphoric "Christian" vision, where the present is valued, interpreted in terms of the eternal hereafter; or it may contribute to an explanation of the remarkable homogeneity of this body of poetry by affirming the connection between the metonymic mode of language and a philosophical continuity in the poems, a pervasive habit of mind that views the poetic subject, whether Christian or pagan, from the standpoint of process, of the present, of this world rather than the next. To argue that the metonymic mode predominates in this poetry (which by no means excludes the coexistent role of metaphor) is to partially explain the readers', or hearers', dynamic involvement with this apparently conventional and formulaic body of poetry. Metonymy does not require, in fact to an extent excludes, the governing, interpreting self, or presence as a determiner of meaning.

As an instance of the Saussurean system of internally referential differences, or of Derrida's field of infinite substitutions, the poem requires that the subject be a function of language, and not the other way around. Saussure and Derrida linguistically recast Peirce's philosophical standpoint that we are "in meaning", not vice versa, or Heidegger's view that language "speaks" us. Chapter 1 asserts that an Old English poem encourages, even demands, that the reader be "in language"—the metonymic impact of the poem upon the reader originates the thrilling and freeing experience of being "spoken."

The notion of abandonment of presence or self, which, it should be noted is an audience-participatory extreme of ancient oral tradition as well as a postmodern characteristic, is modified by the semiotic approach in chapter 2, which more squarely focuses on *Beowulf.* The "semeiotic," the mathematical and logical system of sign analysis of Charles Sanders Peirce, proves particularly illuminating in a discussion of *Beowulf* for several reasons: because Peirce's conception of sign, and his trichotomous divisions of sign categories, are fundamentally connected to his phenomenological categories, the analysis and interpretation of signs always implies a concurrent analysis and interpretation of experience, and of the process of cognition. Peirce takes the subject/self into active consideration. Peirce's terminology can both construct and encompass connections, not only within the signs of the text, but between words and things, between the language of the text and the subject's experience of the text.

Chapter 2 addresses the issue of structure in *Beowulf* from the standpoint of sign interaction. The quicksilver nature of the poem's structure has long foiled logical linear description, primarily because it is essentially nonlinear, describing arcs and circles where persons, events, histories, and stories continually intersect; its individual elements persist, dissolve, and expand in a continuum of resonance and association, offering a poetic structural analogue to interlace design in Anglo-Saxon art. Peirce's concept of sign illustrates the ways in which the sign interaction of the poem mirrors the kinetic dynamic of interlace; the linguistic signs of the poem, through their repetition and interconnection, form networks of indexical association. One sign—for example, a sword—will point "indexically," inevitably, to an "interpretant" (a cognition produced in the mind of the interpreter), such as past enmity; this, in turn, produces another interpretant—for example, future strife—and so on.

Peirce's terminology can evoke the density of the poem's networks of association, and the intensity of cross-signification, a world where words, deeds, and things are viewed as interchangeable. It can describe how the poem's signs seem to set up chain reactions and go around in circles, but it can also conjure the persistent regenerative energy of the movement of interlace, where circles extend into spirals in a process of restless inherent expansion. In Peirce's view semeiosis (poetic, human or otherwise) is a continual process of growth and development, and the meaning of signs inheres in expansion and translation. Although a sign, or set of signs, might possess final determinate meaning, this can be viewed as simply potential; signs grow into determinacy and define their own trajectory of interpretation in tandem with the continually translated and self-examined habits of interpretation of the interpreter. Peirce's concept of sign expands the hermeneutic circle to a spiral (Shapiro, 1983: 10), where sign and interpreter, text and self, exist in an isomorphic and essentially dynamic relation. To return to my overarching metaphor, the distinction between weaver and web is dissolved, each becomes both, reciprocally fused in the act of weaving.

Peirce's emphasis on meaning as process, as a process of continual translation, parallels the linguistic movement of metonymy; it also matches and describes the structure and mode of meaning of *Beowulf*: one might postulate that the entire poem is "about" process—"about" such things as the nature of change (social, moral, and mortal)—perhaps a form of continual questioning and examination of values, heroic and Christian. Chapter 2 seeks to affirm and illustrate the value of a Peircean semiotic approach; Peirce's semeiotic reveals how the signs of the poem work, how they can work upon us, how we are worked by them. It offers a vocabulary and a means of discovery, as it crosses and conflates our categories of experience, and addresses those qualities of the poem that have previously been perceived in art.

Just as chapter 1 postulates that meaning *is* process, and that the reader, the self, is constructed or "woven," identified or "spoken" by the text, chapter 2 also underlines the dynamic aspect of *Beowulf*—the ongoing translation and expansion of sign interaction—but places more emphasis on the interpreter of signs as a functional, contributing element in the process of translation/interpretation. The hermeneutic spiral engages the subject, while the limits and pitfalls of subjectivity are duly acknowledged, incorporated, even programed into the Peircean semeiotic. Chapter 2 does not attempt to analyze or describe the nature of this subjectivity; it is concerned rather with the relationship between reader and text, the ways in which language and the subject are functions of each other. In chapter 3, questions of language/text and its relation to the subject/self, questions about who or what is conditioning the nature of interpretation, become complicated by the issues of desire and gender.

The final chapter continues to trace and parallel the movement of the poem, using gender as the most complex verbal "strand" in the web of interpretation. I have stated that chapter 3 builds on, recasts, and to a degree incorporates the arguments of the preceding chapters, and I shall map out briefly some of the ways in which this progressive complexity develops. The first two chapters reflect on each other: interlace and the metonymic mode image each other, and they both image the metaphor of weaving—the play of difference—in that they share the same capacity for open-ended movement, for indefinite growth and change, a similar resistance to definition and closure. Metonymy offers a linguistic, verbal analogue to the play of difference, while interlace offers a visual, artistic one. The problematic of desire and gender, within and without the text, offers another means of imaging the structure of the web, indeed, the activity of weaving. Introducing the factor of gender, however, raises further questions about the very nature of the web, weaver, and weaving; the characteristic of open-endedness, when viewed through the lens of gender, can become polarized as a positive or negative manifestation of desire.

My introductory quotation from Derrida is taken from his essay "Différance," where he finds the metaphor of weaving the most apt to describe the process and play of *différance*. Central to the inconclusivity and open-endedness of *différance* are the dual attributes of deferring and differing; the lack of closure inherent in the movement of *différance* is a result of continual differing and endless deferral of meaning, which can be doubly evaluated as a "putting off," a lack, a failure to close, or as a triumph of potential, an affirmation of possibility, a refusal to close. In other words, one can see this open-ended "glass" as half-empty or half-full, and both perspectives can be viewed in relation to masculine and feminine modes of desire: the web of *différance* becomes "engendered."

This connection between weaving and gender, and my overall notion of the progressive complexity of the chapters, become clearer if we trace them via the thread of metonymy. The concept of metonymy in its most general sense is concerned with parts, not wholes, with details rather than with the completed picture. Chapter 1 looks at linguistic details without attempting to evaluate how, or even if, they stand in relation to a whole. Chapter 2 looks at how the parts relate to each other, how the details self-connect. Then, to string, or weave, this all together, chapter 3 looks at the question of the directions of the connections, as these are mediated or conditioned by gender. The characteristic of resistance to definition and closure is central to feminist and psychoanalytic examinations of metonymy and its relation to male and female desire. Chapter 3 builds on the earlier linguistic discussion of the mode of metonymy, and its parallel resonance in the mode of interlace, and extends its domain to the psychoanalytic.

In Lacan's view, for example, metonymy and the nature of desire and of interpretation are closely interconnected, if not interchangeable concepts: "Interpretation concerns the factor of a special temporal structure that I have tried to define in the term metonymy. As it draws to its end, interpretation is directed towards desire, with which, in a certain sense, it is identical. Desire, in fact, is interpretation itself" (1981: 176). Lacan, however, focuses on desire as lack, that which leaves a "metonymic remainder . . . an element necessarily lacking, unsatisfied, impossible, misconstrued (*méconnu*)" (154).

The question of direction and conclusion of desire is crucial to both psychoanalytic and feminist viewpoints, although feminist theorists maintain that the perception of metonymy as primarily lack, and therefore necessitating a push for closure and definition, is a perception rooted in masculine patterns of desire: "Since words elicit a desire for meaning, there is a drive to complete the sentence, fully reveal the signification. Yet any 'sentence' can be added to; no sentence is ever completely saturated. The play of metonymy, the forward push to finish signification, to close meaning, creates the impression of veiled signification which Lacan links to the symbolism of the phallus" (Gallop, 1982: 30).

Jane Gallop calls attention to the essentially ambiguous dimension of metonymy in which the differences between male and female sexuality and desire are cast as a question of emphasis, of direction. In the masculine construct, desire is "metonymical impatience, anticipation pressing ever forward along the line of discourse so as to close signification" (30). The feminine emphasis is on the contiguous element, the play of metonymy itself, on "sparks of pleasure ignited by *contact* at any point, any moment along the line, not waiting for closure, but enjoying the touching" (30–31). The feminine perspective here affirms the process of metonymy, the activity of weaving, the possibility inherent in difference: it construes the open-ended "glass" as half-full.

If, as Lacan suggests, desire itself *is* interpretation, the question of direction also has an impact on the process of literary interpretation. Desire *as* interpretation, as process, as it is perceived from a female metonymic standpoint, requires a revaluing of desire as a striving *for*, or toward interpretation; the feminist perspective questions "the impatient economy aimed at finished meaning-products (theses, conclusions, definitive statements)" (Gallop, 1982: 31). The sexual dimension of metonymic ambiguity builds on and expands the chapter 1 discussion of meaning as process or product, metonymy or metaphor, and becomes a further, more intricate means of tracing or paralleling the open-ended movement of the poem. Also, these gender-specific connotations of metonymy will serve to challenge or recast the chapter 2 construction of a collaborative web, an isomorphic relation between text and self. When the web of *différance* is "engendered," new questions are raised about the nature of the text and the self, and of the nature and direction of the desire that produces/creates both. Moreover, the functional problem of working with the premise that desire is interpretation is that it becomes difficult to separate text from reader, to disentangle the workings of desire within the reader from those operating within the narrative.

To repeat a point I made earlier in these preliminary remarks, although the problematic of self raises many interesting questions, I have chosen to pay more attention in this study to desire as/within narrative, to look at the directions and intersections of male and female desire in the poem. The specifically masculine or feminine demands upon the poem from without and the extent to which the reader's desire might shape interpretation of *Beowulf,* or of Old English poetry in general, are issues that merit full and separate investigation, and consequently they will lie for the most part beyond the scope of this study. In focusing on the text, however, and on the connection between text and reader, I do not pretend that this examination of the poem can escape my own desire as reader; by necessity, it will reflect or produce, in some measure, the kind of *Beowulf* I want.

In addition to the open-endedness and resistance to closure of the movements of metonymy and interlace, the intersections of male and female desire in *Beowulf* introduce the strand of paradox into the web of interpretation. The final chapter argues that women have no place in the death-centered, masculine economy of *Beowulf;* they have no space to occupy, to speak from. The system of masculine alliance allows women to signify in a system of apparent exchange, but there is no place for them outside this chain of signification; they must be continually translated by and into the masculine economy.

Although we certainly do not need feminist theory to tell us that *Beowulf* is a profoundly masculine poem, examining the systematic exclusion of women has a number of surprising and illuminating consequences for interpretation, revealing how the women of the poem contribute to the poem's dynamism—here employed in a more literal sense: they deflect or redirect desire away from death and thus affirm its life-related qualities. Death seems to be a pervasive value in *Beowulf;* its privileged position leads to a variety of forms of closure: a continual need for resolution—the hero says, I will do *x* or I will die—and the notion that choice is heroic, inescapable, and reducible to simple binary oppositions. It must be one or the other, and the "other" must always lose—that is, be controlled, assimilated, made the "same"—a process well illustrated in the repetitious reconfiguring of tribal hostilities throughout the poem. Into this binary mode, the women drive a wedge of ambiguity and paradox, providing a discomfiting but nonetheless regenerative glimpse of genuine alterity.

Chapter 3 focuses on three queens in *Beowulf:* the profoundly silent Hildeburh, the language-wielding Wealhtheow, "peace-weaving" with words, and the unmannerly Modthryth, who rends the web of peace with violence. The essentially untenable position of women—one which is predicated on absence and breeds paradox—is exemplified in the primary, if not the only, designated female role of "peace-weaver." As supposedly "active" weavers of lines of connection within the text, these women stand in a specially complex and interesting relation to my overarching metaphor of weaving. They both enact and embody the process of weaving and thus image the play of difference—points I shall be discussing in more detail.

In a culture where war and death are overriding and privileged values, female failure, or nonsignification, is built into the system. One of the consistent characteristics of the peace-weaver in *Beowulf* is her inevitable failure to *be* a peace-weaver; the task is never accomplished, the role is never fully assumed, the woman is never identified. Hildeburh's particularly spectacular failure in the role serves to expose its paradoxical demands, and to indict the system that ostensibly champions her as its cause. The residue of silence left at the end of her disastrous story—a chronicle of her total disappearance into objectification—introduces a temporary paralysis of understanding, a momentary point of standoff when the play of paradox is revealed. Hildeburh's silence is not passive, however; it is an eloquent argument for the "other" as husband, son, and brother, the closest of kin; it affronts, forces a confrontation with ambiguity.

Wealhtheow and Modthryth force similar confrontations with ambiguity, one queen through her language, the other through her mysterious unpredictability. The world of *Beowulf* is poised between language and violence as systems of representation, and in her attempt to use language against and instead of violence, Wealhtheow stands at one of the poem's most important crossroads, embodying the problematic dialectic of a major social transition. The domain of representation opens up, even necessitates, a multitude of possibilities; in affirming the rule of language, this queen also affirms ambiguity and escapes simple binary definition. In its analysis of her speeches and the many possibilities for interpretation they present, the final chapter suggests that Wealhtheow also calls language into question: this woman speaker, who is as absent from language as she is from the masculine symbolic order, temporarily introduces herself as a female subject into the order of language, and her words, like no others in the poem, strip bare the paradoxical core of the whole linguistic project and her relation to it.

Modthryth, too, briefly and yet more violently intrudes herself into the poem's chain of signification. Her rebellion—which is essentially a refusal to be "seen," to be the object of the masculine gaze—constitutes a direct confrontation with the masculine symbolic order. Her violent response to being "seen" reveals the barely displaced violence of the act of staring as appropriation. Modthryth remains a mystery; she is not motivated by love of family (as is the other violent female of the poem, Grendel's mother). Her display of power and violence are self-generated—her rebellion comes from no recognizable source or place, just as her story surfaces in the poem rather abruptly. She utterly rejects a hypothetical identity as a "peace-weaver"; instead, she rends the web apart and actively weaves its antithesis—the "deadly bonds" of death. Although this initially malevolent queen is "tamed" by the love of a good husband, Offa, she remains a mysterious and discomfiting presence, eluding definition in the context of the poem's binary status quo. Modthryth offers a variation on Hildeburh's silent declaration of paradox; she reveals the trace of something we know cannot exist in the world of the poem: the trace of a woman signifying in her own right.

Whatever their relation to the impossible role of peace-weaver, and to the masculine order that negates them as women, queens, wives, or mothers, these three women, "absent" though they are, variously embody the unsettling presence of ambiguity and paradox, and suggest some of the postmodern issues raised by this ancient epic poem. These "weavers" are simultaneously active and passive, present and absent, enacting the creation of the web and created by it; they image the play of difference. We could view their activity of weaving, as Freud might, as an essential failure, an occupation predicated upon and motivated by lack. Although Freud may credit women with the invention of the technique of weaving, regarding it as one of their "few contributions to the discoveries and inventions in the history of civilization" (1933: 132), he hypothesizes that the unconscious motivation for the achievement is shame. Making "threads adhere to one another" (132) is an extension of braiding pubic hair to veil the shame of lack, to conceal the fact of castration. In this view the open-ended "glass" appears completely empty. But I prefer to take a different

LANGUAGE,
SIGN,
AND GENDER
IN *BEOWULF*

1 Language: An Overview in Process

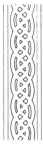

ond on sped wrecan,   spel gerade,
wordum wrixlan

Beowulf, 873–74

to weave words together, and fluently to tell a fitting tale
translated by Kevin Crossley-Holland

and skillfully to adapt an appropriate story, mingling his words
translated by Marijane Osborn

and skillfully to tell an apt tale, to lend words to it
translated by E. Talbot Donaldson

Textual Effects/Affects

The primary concerns of this chapter will be the nature of the language that constructs the Old English poetic text and the effect of this language on the reader, with emphasis on the nature of the reader's response rather than that of the reader. To a large extent, *Beowulf* generates and exemplifies this entity that I have generalized as the "Old English poetic text," but it is also compounded of a variety of references to other poems. This chapter will have a broader, more ambitious, scope than the following ones in that it does not focus solely on *Beowulf,* and hazards some generalizations about Old English poetic diction as a whole; it aims for an overview-in-process, to describe rather than define the mode of this poetic language and the experience of it. As the several translations above indicate, *wordum wrixlan* (exchange/change by or with words)[1] implies process: the phrase applies both to what the Old English poet is doing, and to what we as translators and interpreters are also doing.

1

Before I begin this linguistic and theoretical examination I ask the reader to listen to some rather nontheoretical, nontechnical observations, some impressions that may of necessity reveal the nature of this reader. Allowing for a generous dose of naivete, ingenuous simplicity, and unadulterated enthusiasm, my first impression of Old English poetry is that it is wonderfully immediate; it has an oddly visceral quality that absorbs and moves me; it claims, demands, forges my attention through its power of immediacy and highly spontaneous effect. I am thinking, for example, of the shudder of cold that passages from *The Wanderer* can elicit from myself and from my students. Or the simultaneous fascination and revulsion that draws us inexorably down the path to Grendel's mere. Or, less obviously, the tortuous psychological veracity of Nebuchadnezzar's progress toward faith in *Daniel*. There are many more such examples, and I will maintain, in this chapter, that these few are not solely my own "great moments" in Old English poetry. I shall argue that the powerful, visceral engagement that underlies these impressions, while arguably a representation of my own desire as reader, is also a function of language.

In this naive preamble, I use terms like "immediacy," "spontaneity," or "visceral" tentatively, in an attempt to conjure the peculiar clarity and force that this "dead" language possesses. The equally immediate problem with all these responses, however one labels them, is of course that the linguistic vehicle for this poetry is highly conventional and formulaic, patterned to an extent that might preclude the kind of spontaneous engagement with the text that I am claiming is an essential part of the experience of this poetry.

If we rehearse what we already know, we can describe Old English poetry using a standard list of characteristics or conventions: these include alliteration, repetition, variation, parataxis, use of formulas, word compounds, kennings, antithesis, and understatement. Certain of these conventions are in turn governed and produced by the metrical demands of the poetry.[2] Surveying this array of interconnecting building blocks, one might conclude that the powerful spontaneous experience of the poetry is perhaps at odds with a linguistic system that is very tightly, even rigidly constructed, a disparity voiced by Robert P. Creed when he asks of *Beowulf*, "how can a tissue of formulas, of repeated verses and significant parts of verses, be a great poem?" (98).[3]

Past critics of Old English poetry would by no means agree that the poetry is either immediate or spontaneous in the ways in which I shall attempt to describe. E. G. Stanley's landmark study of Old English poetic diction insists on the high degree of complexity of figurative thought as it is expressed in the poetry, and on the controlling presence of a highly wrought, elaborate poetic diction. Stanley argues that "the finest OE poetic diction is that in which a state of mind or moral concept evokes in the poem the description of a natural phenomenon, associated by the Anglo-Saxons with that mood or moral concept; . . . it is the thought that gives the flower, not the flower that gives the thought" (434). Although Stanley's cerebral, contemplative view-point evokes distance and stasis rather than spontaneity and engagement, his analogy outlines the terms of a distinction that becomes temporarily useful in explaining the coexistence of such a complex and controlled system of diction, at the heart of which lies a core of meaning—that is, the "thought," and the initial perception of the external evidence of this system, or the resultant effect of it, which I shall call the spontaneous and immediate "flower."

Stanley's view requires us to differentiate between the system itself and its actual effect: that is, it introduces a schism between a concept of meaning, which is already in situ, both protected and emblematized by the system, and the vehicle for meaning—form, image, effect—all transitory by-products or "flowers" that might allow access to, but do not generate, thoughts. Stanley's analogy revives an old dialogue in which form and content assume separate functions and stature, one that excludes the problematic of subjectivity and the necessarily shifting middle ground of the reader's response.

The effect of language on the reader or listener has been the province of pragmatic linguists and reader-response critics, and has rarely been a focus for Anglo-Saxonists.[4] Peter W. Travis has argued persuasively for the "natural application to medieval literature" (202) of reader-response or affective criticism in general, and indeed the kinds of questions that reader-response criticism asks of a text might be particularly useful in bridging this ostensible gap in Old English poetry between the nature of the system and that of its effect. Stanley E. Fish suggests replacing the insistent literary critical question, "What does this sentence mean?" with another, more functional question, "What does this sentence do?" (72). Reader-response criticism considers the act of reading to be an inseparable part of textual analysis:[5] Fish, for example, proposes a "method of analysis which takes the reader, as an actively mediating presence, fully into account, and which, therefore, has as its focus the 'psychological effects' of the utterance" (70).

What, then, does the text "do" to the reader of Old English poetry? What are its "psychological effects"? It does not seem adequate to state simply that certain passages of *The Wanderer* produce a shudder of cold, or that others awaken our deepest fears of isolation. Moreover, does what this poetry can "do" depend on the literary and linguistic competence of the reader? These questions must be further complicated by the fact that we do not speak this language; we must labor, as with any foreign language, to piece together a competence that will always be secondary, never second nature, to us. When I posit a reader of Old English poetry, I could assume one who possesses basic knowledge of the language and the ability to read the poems fluently—that is, to do without, for the most part, the help of a dictionary. Or I could also assume one who has learned by rote to the extent that the language of the poetry becomes internalized—much like the way many adults can still recite passages from poems learned in childhood. The literary competence of the reader is an even more nebulous concept. Clearly, the idea that the reader is the sole gauge for determining either meaning or effect has its attendant complications, raising as it must the complex issue of the problematic of self.

While Fish's arguments validate, or at least acknowledge, the importance of the reader's response, he also stresses that "*meaning is an event,* something that is happening between the words and in the reader's mind" (74–75), and that the nature of the collusion between the reader and the text is an essential area for critical examination. The notion, stressed by many writers in literary, cultural, and linguistic terms,[6] that meaning is something that happens, an event enacted by and between reader and text, moves us into less rigorously subjective territory. The semiotic argument of chapter 2 will take up this point by way of Peirce's formulation of self, wherein subjectivity is viewed as an ongoing construction, a continual negotiation between subject and object, between inner and outer worlds. In the linguistic terms of the present argument, the postulation of meaning as a compound function of text and reader gives rise to a dual inquiry: What does the text do and *how* does it do it?

Stanley's analogy is again helpful here. He sees the "flower," or as I would rephrase it, the effect of the poem, as only the appreciable end-product of a complicated and controlled procedure, which is both guardian and repository of meaning, of which the Old English poet is the technical master. The reader of Old English poetry, I would suggest, is able to apprehend the flower and the thought simultaneously. The effect of the poetry is that of a dynamic process of fusion in the mind of the reader of meaning and its representation, of procedure or system, and its end-product. Here I stress the idea of fusion as ongoing process, rather than resolution or crystallization of meaning, and return to the metaphor of weaving described in the introduction, which stresses multifaceted process, continuity, and continual possibility. The structure of the web, which is an especially apt analogue for both the mode of *Beowulf* and our engagement with the poem, facilitates the play of difference, allowing lines of sense to converge and separate freely. What I loosely term "spontaneity" or "immediacy" is a function of this dynamic process of fusion, this simultaneity of impact on the reader. And such an impact, I would further argue, may be explained by postulating that the controlling mode of language in Old English poetry is metonymic rather than metaphoric.

Metonymy: Implications for Interpretation

When Roman Jakobson distinguishes metonymy and metaphor as both linguistic and literary modes, he observes the lack of critical attention paid to metonymy, and the overwhelming critical emphasis on metaphor (258). Studies of metonymy have since proliferated not only in linguistics but in a wide range of subject areas, from semiotic and psychoanalytic criticism to art history and biblical hermeneutics.[7] Most often metonymy and metaphor are still discussed together, a practice I shall follow where useful; the two concepts are necessarily and inextricably linked, one providing commentary on and definition for the other. My use of the concept of metonymy is freely adapted from several theoretical sources and fields, and will be clarified throughout by parallel references to metaphor.

In these general remarks on the implications of metonymy, I have several objectives: to introduce the larger interpretational issues implied by both metaphoric and metonymic modes as a context for the more specific discussion of poems and poetics later in this chapter; to examine the relation of metonymy to the subject as a means of describing the role of the reader and reader-response in Old English poetry; and to begin a discussion of metonymy that will find parallel resonance and expansion in the discussion of interlace in chapter 2, and in the examination of gender in chapter 3.

Jakobson defines the metonymic mode, as it is expressed in language and in a literary text, as characterized by and based on a principle of contiguity (254–59); metonymic "parts" of a text— whether these are grammatical units, images, sentences, themes— are connected by association, by virtue of contiguous placement. In its most basic sense, metonymy is about parts, not wholes; it is the textual practice of looking at details, and of refraining from composing them into unified pictures, which organizing, collocating activity is the proper province of metaphor, a mode based on the principle of similarity. An essential characteristic of the metonymic mode, which differentiates it from metaphor, is its resistance to closure, resolution—in fact, to interpretation in the sense of defining and deciding meaning. The metonymic mode does not offer itself up to interpretation, does not offer some deferred potential insight, or core of meaning, that can be figured out, as it were, through figurative language.

One of the most important issues metonymy raises is that of teleology; the metonymic mode resists, even undermines, either the presupposition (*arché*) or conclusion (*telos*) of finite meaning. My supposition of the controlling presence of metonymy would identify the Old English poetic text in postmodernist terms as a discourse mode without a center, one that functions without a fixed, privileged reference point, or a "transcendental signified"—Derrida's term for that which encompasses and defines all elements of signification within a discourse. In other words, Old English poems are in a sense already deconstructed; their mode of signification is then similar to Derrida's "*freeplay*, that is to say, a field of infinite substitutions in the closure of a finite ensemble" (1972: 260). The poems embody the free interplay of significational elements made possible by the absence of a governing center, or metaphoric overview: the concept of freeplay matches the movement of metonymy. The freeplay of textual elements absolutely rejects reduction or finitude of meaning, requiring a complementary interpretive strategy, "a strategy without finality" (Derrida, 1973: 135), which can be discovered in the irreducible concept of *différance*: "the movement of play that 'produces' (and not by something that is simply activity) these differences, these effects of difference. This does not mean that the *différance* that produces differences is before them in a simple and in itself unmodified and indifferent present. *Différance* is the nonfull, nonsimple "origin"; it is the structured and differing origin of differences" (141).

The concept of metonymy finds considerable expansion and increasingly complex redefinition in *différance*, where meaning is a joint function of the infinite play of differences and of the potential of its infinite deferral. Looking back to the Introduction, metonymy images the metaphor of weaving in that it allows a multiplicity of connections and open-ended, ongoing movement. Looking ahead to the following chapters, it is this aspect of irreducibility and potential—mirrored linguistically in metonymy—that will find resonance in the discussions of interlace and gender.

But, Fred C. Robinson and others might argue, the Old English poem does come to a halt, a conclusion; the text is thematically finite, it takes a stand. In *Beowulf*, for example, Robinson argues that the pagan heroic vision is eventually controlled and subsumed by the Christian. In his discussion of the appositive style in *Beowulf*—which parallels in many respects the juxtapositional principle of metonymy—Robinson demonstrates that "from the smallest element of microstructure—the compounds, the grammatical appositions, the metrical line with its apposed hemistichs—to the comprehensive arc of macrostructure, the poem seems built on apposed segments. And the collocation of the segments usually implies a tacit meaning" (1985: 24–25). The flexibility and tolerance for ambiguity of the appositional style— again, both characteristic of metonymy—may enable the poet to create a temporary double perspective, but in the final analysis ambiguity is controlled and resolved. Although the poet skillfully evokes the dual response of "admiration and regret" (11) for his heathen subject, there can be no doubt that the Christian vision operates as the larger context for the construction of the poem's meaning. While acknowledging incorporation of the pagan vision, the temporary irresolution of apposition is one means by which the poet creates a niche, "a place in his people's mind and language where their ancestors can remain, not with theological security, but with dignity" (59).

In this view, the telos of transitionality eventually subsumes the irresolution of apposition, of co-occurrence. The contiguous coexistence of textual elements is given a logic; parts are made into wholes. Robinson's discussion of the appositional principle marks out some boundaries and intersections of metaphor and metonymy, and prompts some new speculations about an old critical issue — the presence of pagan and Christian elements in Old English poetry. Although I do not propose to address this familiar issue in specific or thematic detail, I want to call attention in these general comments to some implications for interpretation of this so-called dichotomy suggested by the theoretical linguistic constructs of metaphor and metonymy. In summary so far we can say that the metonymic mode suggests a variety of characteristics: flexibility of association and meaning; resistance to conclusion or decisive interpretation; avoidance of interpreting one thing in terms of another in favor of seeing those things for themselves; deferral, which can be indefinite, of resolving meaning into a static or fixed core; emphasis on the here-and-now of immediate perception, on the process and experience of meaning construction rather than on its end-product. If we line these up against characteristics of the metaphoric mode — the movement toward resolution of a juxtaposed dyad into a third overarching, meaning-encompassing element, the location of the experience of interpretation in analysis, in the deferred gratification of achieved meaning, an emphasis on product over process — one could argue that the two modes present a linguistic parallel to cultural modes.

At some risk of bivocalizing culture here, I would suggest that the pagan heroic worldview metonymically emphasizes the individual's present achievement, values the moment salvaged from a transitory life and the inevitable flux of fortune. This immediate world is all there is; it is the ongoing and sole context for interpretation. The Christian vision is essentially metaphoric in that all present meaning is gauged in terms of the hereafter, the promise of punishment or reward, the future effect or meaning of actions; one thing is always seen in terms of another, the physical present is always interpreted in relation to an all-encompassing spiritual reality that dictates and postpones its validation. Whether or not these broad cultural descriptions hold, my point is that the linguistic parallels of metonymy and metaphor remain especially useful in discussing a body of poetry that comes, historically, out of a period of religious and cultural transition, and might therefore demonstrate a kind of linguistic interface of the two modes. My assertion that the metonymic mode predominates in the Old English poetic text by no means does away with the presence of metaphor; it emphasizes a predilection in a relation of coexistence. Looking at a text as a spectrum in which both modes coexist (a point specifically addressed in my discussion of the kenning) is a means of dispensing with the notion of a dichotomy between pagan and Christian elements, of moving this discussion away from the familiar trap of binarism, of replacing the telos of historical transitionality with the simultaneity of literary coexistence.[8]

The difference between Robinson's examination of appositional style and its metaphoric context and my discussion of metonymy is finally a question of emphasis and degree, and of course, desire. Robinson argues, for example, that the Caedmonian "Christianization" of poetic diction resulted not in the restriction or confinement of the pagan poetic tradition, but in greater semantic flexibility and an enhancement of the capacity for ambiguity: "the Christianization of the vocabulary was a matter not of the displacement of pre-Christian meanings by Christian meanings but rather of the extension of pre-Christian meanings to include Christian concepts, and so the words retain vestiges of early meanings while assuming new Christian senses" (1985: 35). Robinson cites as an example the semantic range of a term like *se ælmihtiga*, "the all-powerful being," which belongs in both pagan and Christian contexts.[9] Although Robinson would again insist that semantic ambiguity is controlled by the overall context of the poem, I would suggest that he is also pointing out a development that increases the metonymic capacity of the immediate context. Similarly, although there might be places to "rest" interpretation in *Beowulf*, to halt and say that this means that—Hrothgar's "sermon" to Beowulf, discussed in chapter 2, provides a kind of assemblage of interpretations—my emphasis is on the temporary nature of metaphoric resolution and on the continual metonymic reassertion of the ambiguity of double vision. Like my students, I too find this poem very hard to keep in my mind all at the same time.

Carol Braun Pasternack's discussion of *The Dream of the Rood* offers a further perpective on the issue of metaphoric or metonymic emphasis, one that begins from a more specifically literary or thematic viewpoint and eventually assumes broader cultural and religious dimensions. She looks at the "stylistic disjunctions" in the poem, those places where the poet incongruously juxtaposes thematic elements and switches without warning from one subject or persona to another. Her overview of criticism reveals the secular metaphoric impulse, in that it demonstrates how these various "parts" have been either dismissed, removed, or apologized for in the effort to prove that "all the parts of the poem together coherently express a central theme" (168). Pasternack proposes a different approach, one that recognizes the metonymic construction of meaning through contiguous association. The metonymic parts of the poem, however, are construed as parts of a puzzle connected by an analogical process, one whose logic is divinely discoverable, ultimately metaphoric. The poem's metonymic construction provides the basis for a metaphoric tour de force: the imperfect text lying in pieces becomes an analogue for the imperfect human understanding of the crucifixion, the reader becomes the text awaiting God's interpretation. Whereas in Robinson's formulation, the reader is collocating meaning, resolving the metonymic or appositional dyad into metaphor, in Pasternack's view the metonymic is equated with the secular, worldly parts await heavenly formulation. Excepting the requirement of divine metaphoric intervention, Pasternack's view is not far from my own, in that it allows, in fact insists on, the metonymic irresolution of the *experience* of the text; the reader is in process along with the text, the poem is an experience of the process of understanding and not a conclusion to it.

The shifting cultural and literary territory between the resolution of metaphor and the ambiguity of metonymy makes plain the fact that both metaphor and metonymy are practices that describe both text and reader. As readers we can allow a text to be metonymic rather than metaphoric. To accept the open-ended movement of the text, according to Barthes, is to defer signification and to discover the rewards and freedom of play: "The logic regulating the text is not comprehensive . . . but metonymic; the activity of associations, contiguities, carryings-over coincides with a liberation of symbolic energy" (158). The reader has to be prepared to put meaning "on hold," but in this reciprocal space between text and reader, I shall argue—with the intention of describing more fully reader-response—that the text holds sway. The primarily metonymic Old English poetic text engages, perhaps demands, a metonymic response from the reader.

Robinson, on the other hand, gives the reader final metaphoric sway in that the reader is continually collocating meaning; the appositive—one could also say metonymic—dyad resolves into a third element structured and implied by the theme of the poem. Although Robinson agrees that "there will never be universal agreement on this question" (1985: 6) with regard to *Beowulf*, this mode of constructing meaning in *Beowulf* remains primarily metaphoric; it cannot avoid an element of closure and hermeneutic circularity, and does not take into account the *experience* of ambiguity, or the impact of metonymy, as functions of meaning construction. Also at issue here is the role of the reader, which brings with it the privileging of the subject, of self and presence, and the problem of closure—the entire problematic of Derrida's "metaphysics of presence" wherein the mandate of consciousness as self-presence has historically dictated a series of "transcendental signifiers."[10]

Metaphor, the subject, and the hermeneutic endeavor are intimately and inevitably associated. In his reappraisal of the nature of hermeneutic circularity, Ricoeur proposes that a metaphor is a "work in miniature" (1978: 136) and that "we construct the meaning of a text in a way which is similar to the way in which we make sense of all the terms of metaphorical statement" (142). When we piece together first and second elements of a metaphor, a third "new" or metaphorical meaning results; the important question, Ricoeur asserts, is still *where* the meaning comes from. And here he does not deny circularity, but proposes an expansion beyond a "circle between two subjectivities, that of the reader and that of the author" (145). The subjectivity of projection may be attenuated by a kind of permission, a relinquishment on the part of the reader of a certain kind of reductive control: "the reader understands himself before the text, before the world of the work. To understand oneself before, in front of, a world is the contrary of projecting oneself and one's beliefs and prejudices; it is to let the work and its world enlarge the horizons of my own self-understanding" (145). Although the result is an expansion of self-understanding, the elements of self-reflexivity and appropriation—"the process of making one's own (*eigen*) what was other, foreign (*fremd*)" (145)—remain an inherent part of both the process of hermeneutic interpretation and of metaphorical understanding. Metaphor cannot avoid the metaphysics of presence.

The relation of metonymy to presence, however, is quite different, engaging in Old English poetry not only the issue of the subject but those of collectivity and the oral tradition. The absence of a governing center in discourse also implies the "absence of a subject and the absence of an author" (Derrida 1972: 258).

Despite a traditional cultural investment in the principle of authorship as transcendent genius, as somehow productive of an infinite multiplicity of interpretation, Foucault asserts that the "author is the principle of thrift in the proliferation of meaning" (1984a: 118). Foucault's restrictive view of authorship has particular resonance in the context of oral tradition, especially when proscribed in the following terms: the author "is a certain functional principle by which, in our culture, one limits, excludes, and chooses; in short, by which one impedes the free circulation, the free manipulation, the free composition, decomposition, and recomposition of fiction" (119). Old English poems are almost, but not totally authorless—we do have Cynewulf's signature to prove the rule—and the individually restrictive function of authorship is diminished when the poems, anonymous and otherwise, are placed against the collective backdrop of oral tradition.

Following this line of reasoning, one could posit the oral tradition as a form of governing center for the discourse that is Old English poetry, a center that subsumes to a degree the controlling signification of individual authorship. The concept of a center would consequently reformulate—or deconstruct—itself in terms of continual change, of an ongoing creative process where stories are freely circulated and manipulated, decomposed and recomposed. Although some of the building blocks—those conventions of poetic diction that I enumerated at the beginning of this chapter—may remain relatively static or formulaic, the overall construct is in a state of flux. We continue to formulate an overview-in-process that reproduces the dynamic of weaving, though one that takes us further away from the individual poem and into the realm of cultural abstraction. The notion of freeplay would then extend far beyond the metonymic fabric of a given text/poem; this also raises questions about textual boundaries and textual infinitude, which I will take up in the next chapter. The "finite ensemble" that encloses a field of infinite substitutions may be ultimately a cultural, historical, and not a literary or textual construct. However far one chooses to extend the proper domain of the web of *différance*, the question of the self's relation to it, or absorption by it, remains.

The relation of the reader, or self, to this metonymic playing field instanced by the poetic text is, in John Miles Foley's view, a participatory one encouraged and required by metonymy. Foley views the compositional units of an orally derived text (phraseology, narrative structure, and pattern) as "only libretti for performance":

> They are instanced by synecdoche in the text but their ultimate reality lies in experiencing them as traditional signals that bring their unspoken context into play. In a sense, all such units serve as metonymic cues that assist the reader in formulating and reformulating the work with each reading experience, mediating Hermes-like between the traditional wordhoard and the individual text to support the poet and the reader in their shared task of "raising the great song once more"—even if (nominally at least) for the first time. (Foley, 204)

In this way the reader is "co-creator" of meaning; the self/subject participates in the text/object, and is eventually incorporated by its communality. In Foley's view, meaning is located beyond the text: "the ultimate meaning of unit and work lies outside the text in the collectivity of the wordhoard" (215). Although to some extent we can say that the self is removed and metaphorical control relinquished, in this view meaning may be metonymically accessed, but not metonymically determined—that is, it is not a function of metonymy. In chapter 2 I shall be paying more attention to the conjunction between text and reader, and returning to Foley's notion that the text is "co-created," but my present focus is to locate meaning in the experience of the text. In metonymy, meaning is the process of interpretation, which is the process of experience of the text, and it is this emphasis on meaning as mode *and* experience that distinguishes the concept of metonymy as a means of describing reader-response to Old English poetry.

In order to discover meaning as process and experience of the text, as a function of metonymy, it becomes necessary to reevaluate the relation of reader to text. The aspect of self, or presence as determiner of meaning in any degree, is absent, simply not required, in a purely metonymic structure. As an instance of the Saussurean system of internally referential differences, or of Derrida's field of infinite substitutions, the poem requires that the subject be a function of language, and not the other way around. The nature and function of the self are identified and determined by the nature and function of the system, whether this be language in general or its specific instantiation in a poem. Saussure and Derrida linguistically recast Peirce's philosophical standpoint that we are in meaning, not vice versa, or Heidegger's view that language "speaks" us. I would argue that an Old English poem encourages, even demands that the reader be "in language"; the metonymic impact of the poem upon the reader originates the thrilling and freeing experience of being "spoken."[11]

Wih this emphasis on the processual experience of metonymy—one could imagine being "spoken" here as the process of *being constructed by* the dynamic structuring of weaving, by the operation of the web of *différance* as it is mirrored by metonymy—I want to turn from abstraction to detail and to examine the linguistic building blocks, from tropes to syntax, of this fluid metonymic construct.

When a Kenning Is Not a Kenning

It seems appropriate to begin a discussion of linguistic building blocks of Old English poetic diction with one of its major characteristic tropes, the kenning. I could find no consensus of definition, however, on this central term, and so will set about definition by default. The kenning does not quite function as a metaphor, which is "the figure of speech in which a name or descriptive term is transferred to some object different from, but analogous to, that to which it is properly applicable" (*OED*). The idea of transferral of meaning in the definition of a metaphor is at odds with the idea of substitution of meaning in the *OED* definition of the kenning: "one of the periphrastic expressions used instead of the simple name of a thing."

C. L. Wrenn further differentiates between the merely descriptive epithet or word compound and the "pure" kenning, which must contain a condensed simile: "Thus, for example, *hringed-stefna* . . . is not, strictly, a kenning for 'ship,' but only describes a fact about the ship—namely that it has a ring-shaped prow or stem. But *mere-hengest* . . . is a true 'kenning' for ship, because it implies a simile comparing the ship to a horse (*hengest*), moving over the sea as it does over the plain" (81–82). That several scholars subscribe to either "loose" or "strict" definitions based on degree of metaphoricity is apparent in Ann Harlemann Stewart's survey of critical opinions on the matter (115–118).

Another temporary distinction may be of use here, that between the epithet and its referent, and the epithet and its impact. I would question, for example, how often a reader differentiates between a "pure" kenning and a descriptive epithet, whether the reader stops to make a mental note along these lines: "*mere-hengest* is a condensed simile; the poet does not actually intend to talk about a horse; this is a means, a mere vehicle, for what the poet really wants to talk about—a real ship." It seems more accurate to posit that the reader would take "sea-horse" at face value, and will supply a connotation. In fact the insistent pace set up by meter and alliteration in the poetry can preclude pausing for this kind of interpretative stock-taking, or hesitation in deciding on levels of metaphoricity. (I am aware that the sometimes slow-going process of translation necessary for modern readers of Old English would mitigate against this notion of speed and pace. I am postulating a situation where the modern reader has translated to the point of relatively smooth comprehension. Just how many times *mere-hengest* must be looked up in the dictionary to reach this point, I am not prepared to say; it is a matter for individual assessment.) "Sea-horse" may conjure movement, as it does for Wrenn, or the more literal image of an animal shape. When I have come across "sea-horse" I have seen, perhaps rather fancifully, a sleek, outstretched horse's head, whose mane and the waves of the sea are intermingled.

The important point here is not, however, that individuals see things differently, but that, whether or not one differentiates between a "pure" kenning and a descriptive epithet, the compounds *hringed-stefna* and *mere-hengest* function in the text in the same way: the nature of the effect on the reader is similar. When we read either, we "see" a shape, or witness a certain kind of motion. Each compound evokes an immediate image of how a boat looks, or moves, and pinpoints it momentarily in the reader's visual or imaginative experience.

The reader's response is often one in which the eye and the mind's eye are both called into play. The compound may evoke more than a strictly visual image: *gold-wine* (gold-friend/lord), *feorh-hus* (life-house/body), *woruld-candel* (world-candle/sun), or *swan-rad* (swan-road/sea) are all examples of compounds that mix the visual with the more abstract. They collocate the functional, literal, emotional, and spatial attributes of the "image."

Robinson points out that there is considerable variety in the syntactic, grammatical relationship of one element of a compound to the other, and often "readers or listeners have had to exercise their individual judgment" (1985: 15) in the construction of meaning. Although Robinson emphasizes the "syntactical openness" (16) and flexibility of compounds in *Beowulf*, I have already pointed out in the previous section that he also stresses that the ambiguity generated as a result is controlled, and that context will always be the final arbiter of meaning.

Stewart expresses a similar view in her comparison of riddles and kennings, which she defines in the "strict" metaphorical sense. Although she concedes that both metaphor and metonymy are involved — "the kenning squints" and can produce a "dizzying sense of double vision" (119) — she sees the individual kenning as a variation on a central established archetype. The kenning's referent is revealed as the listener "decodes" the complex message, sorts through the set of possible, related referents grouped together in the poetic tradition, and "recognizes" a meaning that has been there all along (121–28).

Whether meaning is discovered or recognized, the act of interpretation, or making a decision about meaning, is more characteristic of metaphor, and my present concern is metonymy. For the moment, I want to return the focus to the experience and process of meaning construction, and view the compound as an event, a split second of illumination, of individual and imaginative "seeing."

If we see meaning as enacted, as "something that is happening between the words and in the reader's mind," we take the emphasis off a distinction between the epithet and its referent, and the epithet and its impact. We can repose the dual question of what does the epithet do and how does it do it, and postulate a theoretical, linguistic basis for its "psychological effects." Instead of looking at the kenning in terms of metaphor, I suggest that a working definition for the kenning and descriptive epithet (both of which I will call simply compounds) is that applied to the metonym: "a figure of speech which consists in substituting for the name of a thing the name of an attribute of it or something closely related" (*OED*).

The important point of difference between a metaphor and a metonym is that the metaphor always mediates between the reader and a meaning that lies beyond the immediate reference;

meaning is *transferred* to another descriptive term and is always connected to a larger central meaning or point of reference. The metaphor is not self-referential. The metonym, in contrast, is a *substitution* of meaning, an expression used *instead* of the name of a thing. When we come across it in a text, the compound *gold-wine,* for example, substitutes the idea of "lord" for that of "gold-friend" and thus stands as a discrete idea: *gold-wine* does not depend on a central fixed concept of "lord" for meaning. The two ideas exist side by side; they may become connected, even fused together, by association, but each idea is self-referential. As we experience them within the text, the compounds *mere-hengest, hringed-stefna,* and *gold-wine* are not figurative in the sense that a metaphor is, because they are not founded on an act of interpretation. We do not need to look beyond the image for its complete meaning, but accept its immediate impact—take it at face value.

Focusing attention on the reader's experience of metonymic effect attenuates but by no means does away with the problem of a certain arbitrariness inherent in distinguishing between the metonym and metaphor. Although I argue that the metonymic principle *predominates* in Old English poetry, this by no means eliminates the role of metaphor; nor is it necessary, or even feasible, to accept an either/or classification of linguistic and poetic modes. Having to decide on one or other mode returns us to the problem of how to reconcile the highly conventional, sometimes rigidly formulaic, nature of Old English poetic diction with its spontaneous and often thrilling effect upon the reader— and perhaps this "problem" is not one at all, but merely a paradox of coexistence that dizzies our linear perception. Instead of setting up a false choice between modes, one can pose the question of how do the classifications of metaphor and metonymy relate to the *experience* of the poem, as opposed to the contemplation of the text, or to the single instance in the poem of a compound used perhaps dozens of times within the poetic tradition?

A less arbitrary approach to the distinction between metaphoric and metonymic modes is to view the text as a spectrum that encompasses both, and establishes an internal dynamic that gives greater or lesser emphasis to one mode. Michael Shapiro underscores the notion of the text as a spectrum in his examination of the essential interrelatedness of the two modes, and of the "life-cycle" of tropes. While Shapiro follows Jakobson in basing all tropes on a relationship of either contiguity (metonymic) or similarity (metaphoric), he introduces a third element of value, or ranking, the degree to which one relation supersedes the other. "In metonymy, the referential dimension predominates over the significational, whereas in metaphor this dominance relation is inverted" (1983: 198). The terms "referential" and "significational" here correspond to denotation and connotation, or external meaning (physical objects and events) and internal meaning (their conceptual counterparts). Shapiro uses an example from Zola, "loud voices wrangled in the corridors," to demonstrate the external, referential focus of metonymy: "the hierarchy of semantic features or range of connotations remains unchanged . . . 'voice' stands for itself in the Zola example as well as for 'person' but *not vice versa*. The fact that 'voice' retains its meaning while simultaneously referring to something other than itself is precisely one of the *differentiae specificae* of metonymy over and against metaphor" (199). The internal, significational focus of metaphor, on the other hand, makes the relation between the metaphoric term and its usual referent "discontinuous or indirect," more difficult to grasp in an immediate sense. Shapiro's example, Pascal's "man is a thinking reed," shows how the meaning of "reed" per se disappears and becomes temporarily included in the meaning of "man."

Old English compounds like "ring-prow" or "gold-friend" parallel Zola's "loud voices"; the dominance of external reference contributes to what I have been calling the spontaneity of the effect of the image within the poem. Using the example of the metonymic *pars pro toto* "sail" for "ship," Shapiro remarks that "no wonder the part chosen to represent the whole is the most prominent one; prominence is, after all, a relation of rank. One might even assert that the choice of the item singled out in metonymy is perceptually and/or cognitively well-motivated (natural)" (1983: 201). This closeness to cognition, a form of reproduction of the passage of the eye and movement of the imagination, underlines the "primal character of metonymy as well as the greater immediacy of its link to perception as compared to metaphor" (202). Shapiro's linguistic argument for the primacy of metonymy, while providing some support for my previous use of terms like "visceral" and "immediate" to describe my response to the poetry, is also reflected in psychoanalytic constructions of metonymy.[12]

We can also observe a spectrum of gradations in the dominance of external reference in compounds such as *feorh-hus* (life-house/ body), *hamora laf* (leavings of hammers/sword), and *hron-rad* (whale-road/sea). Are these incipient, some might say full-blown, metaphors, requiring a substantial interpretive act on the part of the reader? Another issue raised here is how or where to draw the line between the literal and the figurative, between fact and figure. Over fifty years ago H. C. Wyld was puzzling over how "full of life" were the phrases of this poetry so often considered bound by convention; he suggested that the imagery retains its vitality because "the poet does not merely feel that things are *like* something else, his mind bridges the gulf, and he sees the two things as identical" (83).

Stanley later takes up the same point; although he argues for the carefully controlled use of devices and highly developed capacity for figurative thought evident in Old English poetry, he also insists on the fusion, or occasional confusion, between fact and figure: "In a number of cases the symbolic is so closely interwoven with the factual element in the description that it is not possible to say which is foremost in the poet's mind" (439). One particularly interesting and complex example of this is the *Genesis B*-poet's use of the term *wæstm* (fruit, form, result), which recurs and links together the stages of Eve's fall in a powerful fusion of literal and symbolic consumption and its factual and spiritual consequences.[13]

Stanley also warns that a "modern reader accustomed to scientific precision is in danger of importing the neat distinction of fact and figure into an age that did not know it or need it" (422). Division of fact and figure is a characteristic of the metaphoric mode, while fusion is more characteristic of the metonymic. In fact, Stanley's description of how Old English figurative language can work upon the reader borders on an analogy for the metonymic process: "Few will deny that with the old poets the processes of nature may be symbols of their moods: but it is not the flower that gives the thought; with the OE poets it is the thought that gives the flower. And the flower that is born of the mood may take on sufficient concreteness to appear capable of existence without and outside the mood" (427). Fact fuses with figure to allow the reader's simultaneous apprehension of the flower and the thought.

The metonymic nature of the compound not only encourages the spontaneity of the reader's response but also the dissolution of the tension generated by analytical distinctions between fact and figure, or between the epithet and its referent, and the epithet and its impact. In fact, the experience of metonymy makes the question of how or where to draw the line between the literal and the figurative redundant or temporarily irrelevant. Incipiently metaphoric compounds like *hron-rad* or *feorh-hus* still retain their metonymic impact, although the dominance of external reference may be diminished. The compound retains its self-referentiality in its immediate context; it comprises a moment of "seeing," a momentary fusion of a variety of aspects in combination, whether visual, spatial, emotional, or literal, which is facilitated by the metonymic fabric of the text as a whole. Other grammatical and syntactic aspects of metonymy in Old English, which I shall discuss, fix the metonymic effect of the compound within the text.

In contemplating a certain passage, the poem as a whole, or several poems within the Old English poetic tradition, we might become more aware of the metaphoric or figural nature of a given image; some images, *hamora laf*, for example, may require more "unraveling," or a quicker assimilation of metaphoric meaning; we might come across the more self-evident "ring-prow" several times, or collocate it eventually with a dozen other epithets for ship within the whole poetic tradition in a more gradual apprehension of its figurality. It is a question of degree. "It is the contextual locus, or more fully, the necessary presence of the contiguity relations facilitated by the context that allows the figural meaning of a metonymy to be perceived and understood as such" (Shapiro, 1983: 12). In other words, although we might understand the eventual significance of the compound as metaphoric in its larger context—which raises the issue of final "resolution" of meaning—we experience it metonymically in its immediate context.

All forms of metonymy, according to Shapiro, contain the potential for "sliding into metaphor" unless fixed or "localized" in a text; "similarly, metaphors are geniunely resistant to lexicalization (fading) only when firmly anchored to the literary text" (203–4). This "slide" is part of the movement inherent in Shapiro's concept of the "life-cycle" of tropes, in which tropes consistently change and evolve through time; metonym becomes metaphor, which in turn becomes "lexicalized," an idiom or a part of ordinary vocabulary, until or unless a poet comes along and revives the original power of the trope. Examples of this development abound in our everyday language: "hood" (or "bonnet") of a car, or Shapiro's example, "head" of a committee, which functions simultaneously as a metonym and a metaphor. However, the *pars pro toto* usage is overtaken by the metaphoric analogy of the dominance of the head over the rest of the body, and thus "head" also demonstrates "the principle that metonymy tends strongly to be superseded by metaphor" (204). The power and effect of the metaphor or metonym is "either crucially dependent on and/or significantly enhanced by textual locus" (204) and, I would add, by the mode of fixing it within the text. I shall argue in the next section that the overall structural, syntactic, and thematic context for the compound in the Old English poetic text is also primarily metonymic, thus ensuring and enhancing its metonymic function and effect.

The commonplace observation that an often repeated or hackneyed word or phrase can be novel and startling in its poetic context has particular resonance in Old English poetry. The Old English poet is working with and reworking a fairly stable set of fixed elements. He is a kind of juggler; like Hrothgar's scop in *Beowulf,* he is continually engaged in a process characterized by the phrase *wordum wrixlan.* We might even say that his collection of images and formulas, bound within the constraints of alliteration, are beyond metaphor: they have already become lexicalized, a part of the ordinary language of the Old English poetic tradition, made "ordinary" by the degree of its accepted conventionality. What makes these poems so compelling must therefore lie in the arrangement, the contextual fixing, of these familiar elements. The spontaneity and immediacy of Old English poems is a result not only of the poet's craft in juggling but also of the metonymic force that characterizes the language he crafts.

Metonymy in Action

What can the principle of metonymy tell us about the nature of the reader's response to the Old English poetic text? How can it specifically describe the experience of being "in language," of being "spoken?" In this section I want to address these questions by looking in more detail at passages from *Beowulf* and other Old English poems. My first choice is a passage that has been used many times to prove a variety of points of view, though I see this controversiality as a particular indicator of the passage's power to generate difference, as testimony to its dynamic potential. Lines

210–29 from *Beowulf* describe the hero's journey to Denmark; although some critics cite this passage as one of the most conventional and formulaic in the poem, it also provides a good introductory example of the metonymic compound in action, which in turn opens out to a broader view of the metonymic principle at work.[14] The passage highlights an important factor that facilitates and contributes to the metonymic effect of the compound: the pace of the poem, determined by meter and alliteration and also by the speed and intensity with which compounds, images, and ideas follow each other. I use Kevin Crossley-Holland's literal gloss because it is particularly blunt and uncompromising, and manages to convey at least some of the excitement of the original:

> Fyrst forð gewat;   *flota* wæs on ýdum,
> *bat* under beorge.   Beornas gearwe
> on *stefn* stigon, — streamas wundon,
> sund wid sande;   secgas bæron
> on bearm *nacan*   beorhte frætwe,
> guðsearo geatolic;   guman ut scufon,
> weras on wilsið   *wudu bundenne.*
> Gewat þa ofer wægholm   winde gefysed
> *flota famiheals*   fugle gelicost,
> oð þæt ymb antid   oþres dogores
> *wundenstefna*   gewaden hæfde,
> þæt ða liðende   land gesawon,
> brimclifu blican,   beorgas steape,
> side sænæssas;   þa wæs sund liden,
> eoletes æt ende.   Þanon up hraðe
> Wedera leode   on wang stigon.
> *sæwudu* sældon, — syrcan hrysedon,
> guðgewædo;   Gode þancedon
> þæs þe him ýðlade   eaðe wurdon.   (210–24)

> Time went forth: *floater* was on waves,
> *boat* under cliff.   Warriors eager
> on *prow* climbed, — streams eddied,
> sea against sand;   men bore
> into bosom of *ship*   bright armour,
> war-gear splendid;   men out shoved,
> warriors on wished-voyage   *wood (well)bound*
> Went then over wave-sea   by wind hastened
> *floater foamy-necked*   to bird most like,
> until at due time   of second day
> *curved prow*   journeyed had,

> that the voyagers   land saw,
> sea-cliffs shining,   cliffs steep,
> wide sea-nesses;   then was sea crossed,
> journey at end.   Thence up quickly
> Geats' men   on shore stepped,
> *sea-wood* moored, — mail shirts rattled,
> battle-garments;   God (they) thanked
> because for them wave-paths   had been easy.

I have italicized eight references to the sailing vessel, occurring in the space of fourteen lines. Before the actual journey is underway, the vessel is referred to in varied but neutral terms: floater, boat, prow, and ship. When the journey begins, the vessel assumes more prominence and the image moves into focus; in fact, it solidifies as the warriors are pictured aboard "wood (well)bound." As the wind picks up, the image of the vessel changes again: the still *flota* of line 210 breaks into movement with the addition of *famiheals*. Only the last two references to the vessel are compounds, but as these follow in the rapid succession of images, they have a metonymic immediacy of impact. We switch from a view of the twisted prow in motion (arising, as it seems to, from a "foamy neck"), to the compound sea-wood, which Crossley-Holland equates with the weight and solidity of the Geats's armor (126–27n). The equation suggests a return to stillness, a sort of landlocked thump that ends the vessel's spurt of movement. One can see a similar pattern in the five references to the sea: waves, streams, sea, wave-sea, wave-paths. The ship, though moored, is associated with movement, "on waves"; the next two references are details of the poet's composite perspective where lots of different things are happening: men are moving around and loading up, and while smaller streams eddying around the ship indicate potential movement, the image of sea against sand connotes stasis. In full sail, the vessel crosses a billowing wave-sea, and at the end of the journey the wave-paths of the sea suggest an image for a way traveled, a sea-route carved out and negotiated.

I have been focusing on the rapidity of changing perspectives offered by this succession of separate and compound images. The dynamism of this passage is also a result of the poet's use of variation, parataxis, and alliteration, conventions employed so skillfully that any intrusive hint of contrivance or artistic mechanism vanishes. But the effect of the passage is also a function of metonymy, of the general principle of contiguous placement: as the metonymic compound remains self-referential, so does the metonymic idea—the phrase or group of words that can carry independent meaning. Images and ideas are in a contiguous relation to each other: they are placed side by side in a text but remain essentially discrete, connected only by association and proximity.

Delineated as it is by meter, by the devices of variation, parataxis, and alliteration, the very nature of the half-line division in Old English poetry functionally supports the proposition that the poetry is metonymic rather than metaphoric in structure, that associations are made by contiguity rather than comparison. Often the half-line conveys discrete sense and can be seen as a completed "capsule" of information. Crossley-Holland's literal gloss of the *Beowulf* passage helps to make this point clear. If I were to write out lines 217–18 in "good" English sentence order, the result would be something like this: "then the foamy-necked floater, which was most like a bird, went over the wave-sea hastened by the wind." The particular problem with this rendering is the imposition of an ordered, linear, grammatical sequence that distorts and diminishes the passage's effect. Even the addition of definite and indefinite articles, which Robinson reminds us are not necessary in Old English (1985: 39), inhibits the potential of the original by introducing an arbitrary and reductive specificity. The grammatical awkwardness and choppiness of Crossley-Holland's version convey more of the virtues of the original—the tension, the sense of movement, the open-ended, nonlinear development of ideas. His version retains four distinct ideas or information "capsules," corresponding to the half-line divisions. Impressionistically speaking, these are: the going, the wind, the ship, and the bird, which are connected, and which we as readers connect, through association by contiguity.

An appropriate, and perhaps increasingly apparent analogy for what is "happening between the words and in the reader's mind" is that of film. The analogy has been drawn before by Old English scholars, but it is especially useful in illuminating the metonymic process.[15] Lines 217–18 might be cinematographically translated as four shots, or different angles, following each other in rapid succession; the shots would convey four images or representations of the four ideas of going, wind, ship, and bird. The organization of these shots or angles in the mind of the reader (that is, the ordering of experience that emerges as the motivation and result of my remodeled version of Crossley-Holland's literal gloss) is less important, indeed less *appropriate,* than a capitulation to the spontaneity and immediacy of their effect.

Association of ideas through contiguity is facilitated by the absence of an ordered, grammatical sequence—also described as the conventional use of parataxis in Old English poetry. A. L. Binns calls attention to the dearth of techniques of grammatical subordination, and praises the effect that this deficiency produces. He argues that the nongrammatical organization of ideas is not an accident, nor poor craftsmanship, and shows how the imposition of ordered syntax in translation "lacks the immediacy" of the poet's original arrangement (127). In his commentary on lines 1285–87 in *Beowulf* Binns points out the poet's preference for a string of phrases that are grammatically unsubordinated instead of a simple noun, and also offers a demonstration of the virtues of metonymy:

Old English poetic style *substitutes* this array of fragmentary, immediate impressions for the word "battle," keeps everything on the same line and resolutely refuses to analyse the phenomenon into kernel and adjectival trimmings. It is not simply a substitution of strongly stressed nouns for weaker verbs and adjectives as implied by the examples used by [E. G.] Stanley, but an embodiment, close-up and breathless because unsubordinated, of the impressions of battle, effective as a more sophisticated abstraction cannot be. (128–29)

Binns's insistence on the lack of closure, or resistance to resolution of meaning inherent in this aspect of Old English poetic style, points toward metonymy. Randolph Quirk approaches the question of parataxis from a more metaphoric standpoint; rather than carrying discrete emphasis, or the immediacy of metonymic impact, instances of lack of grammatical connection provide "an effect which can be achieved not only because the particular type of lexical connexion is already established in the poem, but also because the whole metrical tradition has, as we have seen, established an expectation of lexical connexion" (6). In this view, the tradition programs the reader. The effect of agrammaticality, along with that of "incongruous collocations" (Quirk's term for unlikely instances of variation, disconnected ideas being placed side by side in the text with no grammatical apology or justification), can be gauged only by measuring them against the norms established by the text as a whole, and dictated by metrical tradition. As in Robinson's argument, context is the vehicle for

interpretation, enabling the reader to arrive at a grounded, ana-
lytical conclusion about meaning. While I agree that Old English
poems positively reverberate with resonances both internal (within
the text) and external (within the tradition), I return to my
emphasis on the process and experience of meaning construction
and the importance of the actual effect on the reader: the momen-
tary surprise, disorientation, disruption, the sense of being in a
limbo of meaning (from a metaphoric point of view), and the
deferral of resolution occasioned by grammatical aberrations or
incongruous collocations are all facets of the metonymic presenta-
tion of ideas.

The principle of contiguity gives rise to incongruities of several
kinds; it can ignore the rules of grammatical association and
thwart expectation of sequential order. In fact, the metonymic
mode of language allows for more flexibility and diversity, and
greater freedom of association of ideas: "Following the path of
contiguous relationships, the realist author metonymically di-
gresses from the plot to the atmosphere and from the characters to
the setting in space and time" (Jakobson, 255). Jakobson's "realist
author" is chronicling experience as it unfolds, reproducing the
passage of the eye and the movement of the imagination. A ship
may be a "ring-prow" at one point, and then a "sea-horse" a few
lines later; the cross in *The Dream of the Rood* is an alternating
vision of hope and despair: at one moment it is a jewel-studded
ornament, at the next it sweats blood as a reminder of torture and
ancient strife. These images occur in the here-and-now of the
reader's perception; each is a momentarily accurate representa-
tion of the way perception flickers and changes. This is not to
confuse the idea of modern stream-of-consciousness narrative
with Old English poetic techniques; the construction of the
narrative is far too conventional for that, and one must always
keep in mind the fact that the poet may have employed the term
"ring-prow" at least a hundred times. But this does not prevent
the reader from "seeing" it afresh in context. Jakobson's notion of
realism is tied to the premise that the reader's apprehension of
reality in a metonymic text is, like the reality itself, constantly
changing, fluid, composite, many-faceted, and in some respects
essentially disordered, not conforming to externally imposed
linear, chronological expectations.

Jakobson's observation on metonymic digression finds interest-
ing and apt parallels throughout Old English poetry, and I offer

here just a few examples. The principle of contiguity may be readily detected in two poems as different as *The Wanderer* and *Christ and Satan*. Consider these lines from *The Wanderer*:

> wod wintercearig   ofer waþema gebind,
> sohte sele dreorig~~sinees~~ bryttan   (24–25)[16]
>
> went winter-sad   over binding of the waves,
> sought hall-dreary   a giver of treasure[17]

The realism of these lines is founded on the momentary accuracy of perceptions of mood and physical environment as these occur to the mind's eye or appear to the eye. The compounds *seledreorig* and *winter-cearig* evoke a variety of images associated with loneliness and desperation, and do much to involve the reader in the stark reality of the exile. But this reality is also evoked by the rapidity and intensity with which images and ideas succeed each other. Pace is established by meter and alliteration, and by the range of information offered by the four half-line capsules. The poet metonymically progresses to present mood, location, and intention of the wandering exile within a very short space. *The Wanderer* is of course one of the most loved and critically acclaimed of all Old English poems; the poem abounds with examples of similar metonymically evocative power:

> Warad hine wræclast,   nales wunden gold,
> ferdloca freorig,   nalæs foldan blæd.   (32–33)
>
> Exile-path attends him,   not twisted gold,
> heart-coffer frozen,   not earth's glory.

What has twisted gold to do with a frozen heart? The absence of grammatical relationships strengthens the incongruity of these contiguous images, and enhances the contrastive sweep of ideas — from enclosure in solitude, to the absence of remembered beauty, to the stultified emotions, to the lack of earth's abundant bounty — all of which crowd and invade and comprise the essentially displaced reality of the exile.

It is equally interesting to look at some lines from a rather less popular and less accessible religious poem, *Christ and Satan*. In this passage Satan is describing and lamenting his fallen condition in hell:

> "Nu ic eom dædum fah,
> gewundod mid wommum;   sceal nu þysne wites clom

> beoran beornende   in bæce minum,
> hat on helle,   hyhtwillan leas."   (155–58)[18]

> "Now I am stained by deeds,
> wounded with evil;   now I must this fetter of torment
> bear burning   on my back,
> hot in hell,   without hoped-for joy."

There are no descriptive compounds that evoke strictly visual images in this passage; only one compound, *hyhtwillan*, is used at all. But the lines compare to those from *The Wanderer* from the point of view of intensity and density of information. The ideas of physical pain, mental anguish, defilement, captivity, and hopelessness are all condensed in a short space. All these ideas are associated because they are aspects of Satan's reality, but their contiguous relationship allows them to remain discrete, while allowing for quantity, diversity, and complexity of information. The passage initially conflates the real and the psychological, effectively obscuring the distinction between literal and spiritual torment: Satan is stained and wounded not by blood or weapons, but by his own sins. We cannot, and need not, decide on the exact nature of the "fetter" that restricts him. Remembering Stanley's remarks, the modern reader need not impose clear distinctions between fact and figure, because the metonymic structure obviates, makes irrelevant, such a decision. The last line contains two separate ideas: *hat on helle* indicates physical sensation and location, and this information is immediately followed by *hyhtwillan leas*, indicating a mental state. While alliteration binds these separate ideas forcefully, so that heat and hopelessness resound with parallel intensity,[19] their contiguous relationship allows them a discrete, metonymic immediacy as well. The gamut of possibilities allowed by the metonymic presentation of ideas in this passage vividly reproduces Satan's agonized, composite reality.

The greater flexibility of association characteristic of the metonymic mode often occasions a disruption of linear chronology and of the congruity of ideas. It has become a critical commonplace to observe that Old English poems seldom provide a neat beginning, middle, or end to satisfy or organize the reader. Furthermore, in the middle of discussing one thing, the Old English poet might insert something else apparently unrelated. Quirk's notion of "incongruous collocations" extends throughout the poetry at many structural levels: at the level of the single phrase or several lines—which my examples so far have addressed—to a sizeable chunk of text with discrete thematic content, an entire digression.

Digressions are an essential characteristic of the Old English poetic text, but are especially prominent and have an interesting critical history in *Beowulf.* In the past these wayward metonymic "parts" or details have been variously contorted to produce wholes, or unified pictures of the poem (in much the same way, for example, that Pasternack describes the critical history of stylistic disjunctions in *The Dream of the Rood*). Now that the digressions are considered legitimate, they are seen as integral, organic "parts" of a whole nonetheless, and the question arises of which detail is noticed or privileged, which part is more or less integral to the whole. Chapter 3 will take up these issues with particular reference to the digressions concerning women; here I want to return to a nonevaluative emphasis on the discrete nature and effect of these larger metonymic building blocks.

Metonymic placement of digressions can do interesting things to our sense of time as readers of *Beowulf.* In the middle of the dragon fight, for example, the poet stops the action abruptly to tell us the history of the sword Wiglaf is about to use. This interrupts the narrative sequence, jolts and rearranges the reader's attention. We learn that the ancestral sword was taken by Wiglaf's father from the dead body of the brother of the Swedish king, and it thus serves as a present reminder in the narrative of a past feud with the Swedes, which will cause the future destruction of Beowulf's people after he is dead.

The effect of the contiguous placement of the digression in the main narrative is to give the reader an almost simultaneous perception of past, present, and future. Time is telescoped into a continuum of present experience, as one event is associated, even identified in the metonymic mode of substitution, with the other. The dynamics of this process of association, and the complex intersectioning of time frames in *Beowulf,* will be discussed in greater detail in chapter 2. My present brief glimpse at this digression serves to focus on its effect, which is a heightening of immediacy, a sharpening and enlargement of the reader's perception facilitated, even forced, by this contiguous placement of apparently disparate ideas.

The story of Wiglaf's sword is one of the recognizably discrete digressions in the poem, but it is worth noting that the metonymic

juxtaposition of time frames and the almost casual disruption of
ordered chronology can be found in much shorter sequences. To
cite but a few examples: the future destruction of Hrothgar's hall
is mentioned alongside its present lofty and imposing appearance
(1181–85); Grendel's future defeat is juxtaposed to his savage
exultation and expectation of bloodshed as he enters Heorot (730–
36); Beowulf's instructions for a new shield to protect him against
the dragon are set next to a reminder of his future defeat and soon
followed by reminders of his past strength and exploits (2336–53).
Similar juxtapositions can occur at the phraseological level, as we
have seen in earlier examples.

Following a somewhat metonymic sequence in my own argu-
ment, I move once again away from *Beowulf* and offer one final
illustration from *Daniel,* which incorporates the metonymic juxta-
position of time frames and the contiguous placement of dispa-
rate ideas. In a moving passage, which describes the conclusion of
Nebuchadnezzar's exile and madness, the poet brings the king's
past and present together; the result is a poignant mixture of
irony and pathos:

> Seofon winter samod   susl þrowode,
> wildeora westen,   winburge cyning.
> Ða se earfoðmæcg   up locode,
> wilddeora gewita   þurh wolcna gang.   (620–24)[20]

> Seven winters together   he endured torment,
> wilderness of wild beasts,   king of the festive city.
> Then hardship's son   looked up,
> companion of wild beasts,   through the clouds' passing.

The time frame switches rapidly from a span of years prolonged
by suffering to a momentary glance upward, from a past perspec-
tive of urban prosperity laid next to a vision of bestial deprivation.
Nebuchadnezzar's conversion is no sudden miracle; in the hands
of the Old English poet this Bible story loses its aura of fable or
parable and becomes a psychologically accurate description of a
man's changing consciousness.[21] In this short passage, we can see
one reason for this kind of realism, or closeness to actual cogni-
tion, in the simultaneity of perspective inherent in the metonymic
mode. The king's past and present are layered, as it were, in
contiguous, not derived or teleological, association; the past re-
flects and compounds the present; it is a part of it, not an
explanation for it. In the Old English account, the reformed king

carries his experience with him back to Babylon; his conversion is no instant metamorphosis, as it is in the Bible, but a present realization of past suffering and learning.

The passage from *Daniel* ends this brief, eclectic survey of examples of metonymy in action, and brings me back to the beginning of this chapter. There I hoped to show that the powerful effect of this poem—what I called its "tortuous psychological veracity"—was not solely a representation of my own or a single reader's desire, that such an effect might be explicable within the theoretical linguistic framework of metonymy. Whether or not I have persuaded readers that they are metonymically "spoken" by this poetry, the issue of desire remains. In Lacan's psychoanalytic construct outlined in the Introduction, desire itself is identical with the activity of interpretation—which premise makes it difficult to separate text from reader, to disentangle the workings of desire within the reader from those operating within the text. The questions remain of whether the Old English poetic text is metonymic, whether I want it to be metonymic, or whether I have any choice in the matter, if, as Lacan insists, the operation of desire is metonymic—that is, that which is lacking, incomplete, unfulfilled. I have no ready answers; I have stated that this is not a book about deciding meaning, but rather how meaning is decided, and how the reader participates in the process of meaning construction. I propose instead to continue to raise these questions from different theoretical viewpoints in the following chapters, in an attempt to refine and expand them, to weave a more complex context for the practice and process of interpretation, one that aims to be consonant with the difference of the Old English poetic text.

In the next chapter, I want to examine a more collaborative dynamic between text and reader. In terms of the metonymic argument of this chapter, I will analyze some of the ways in which we are "spoken" by "permission." This chapter has looked at metonymic "parts" of language, at linguistic details, without attempting to evaluate how, or if, they stand in relation to a whole. Chapter 2 will consider more specifically how the parts of *Beowulf* relate to each other, how the details self-connect, and how the reader is engaged in this process. The linguistic principle of metonymy, of open-ended process, will be translated into semiotic terms; the next chapter analyzes the dynamic semiosis of *Beowulf,* where the coherence of signs matches the restless, inherently expansive mode of interlace in Anglo-Saxon art. Interlace and the metonymic mode share the same capacity for indefinite growth and change, a similar resistance to definition and closure.

The question of the relation of the single metonymic compound to the entire poetic tradition has been raised throughout this discussion, initially in the context of how the spontaneity and immediacy of the instance in the text can coexist with the rigid demands of a highly conventional, formulaic tradition. I have already pointed out that this same tradition might not function as a governing center, but rather that it can be seen as continually deconstructing and reconstructing itself, and that as an encompassing "finite ensemble" for the "freeplay" of infinite substitutions, the tradition that encompasses the text might have cultural and historical boundaries. But what of the metonymic instance in the individual poem? Where does the individual text begin and end, and how do we as readers mark out its boundaries? Chapter 2 also takes up the issue of the finitude, or otherwise, of the individual text by examining *Beowulf* from an interartistic, semiotic perspective.

Like metonymy, interlace is another analogue of weaving, another image of process, which is designed to trace or parallel aspects of the complex movement of the poem. The Peircean semiotic analysis of the following chapter will add another verbal strand to this textual and critical web; it will build on and expand the construct of metonymy, and will engage the reader in a collaborative web of interpretation.

2   Swords and Signs: Dynamic Semeiosis in *Beowulf*

A sign is something by knowing which we know something more

Charles Sanders Peirce

Interlace, Text, and Sign

Chapter 1 suggested that we can understand the interpretive impulse toward, or resistance against, making parts into wholes in terms of metonymic or metaphoric principles motivating the text or the reader. *Beowulf* and *Beowulf* scholarship represent a curious disjunction in this regard—the poem stubbornly resists the impulse, while its critics have persistently enacted it. The essentially non-Aristotelian narratological structure of the poem has usually been viewed as a problem to be solved, and the impulse to unify its disparate parts has pervaded *Beowulf* scholarship in many guises. When Klaeber described the structure of *Beowulf* in terms of "lack of steady advance," he pinpointed, somewhat euphemistically, the problem facing readers searching for unity. If the author "does not hesitate to wander from the subject," by what means can the reader identify that subject clearly, or trace a coherent line of progress along the poem's "rambling, dilatory path?" (Klaeber, lvii). Klaeber's question puts the burden of responsibility on the reader for discovering a whole out of these unruly parts, but it does not call attention to the possibility that the desire for unity originates and terminates within the reader.

The search for unifying structural principles in *Beowulf* has gone hand in hand with an overall critical desire to legitimate its equally unruly subject matter. And both desires, Frantzen points out, belong to the reader and not to the poem; they are part of the process by which critics have "written" the poem for themselves.[1] Tolkien's enormously influential essay on monsters and critics begins this dual push for legitimization: "After Tolkien," writes Frantzen, "a *Beowulf* without thematic coherence became as unthinkable as a *Beowulf* without dignified subject matter" (1990). It instigated one of the most prevalent structural and thematic constructions of the poem's unity, a dualistic vision of the poem as a series of contrasts and oppositions, and one that engages my previous discussion of metonymy and the following semiotic analysis. Tolkien summarizes this point of view in his response to Klaeber: "But the poem was not meant to advance, steadily or unsteadily. It is essentially a balance, an opposition of ends and beginnings. In its simplest terms it is a contrasted description of two moments in a great life, rising and setting; an elaboration of the ancient and intensely moving contrast between youth and age, first achievement and final death" (34–35).

Tolkien's view of opposition as a structural principle has recently been recast and expanded by Robinson's discussion of the appositive style in *Beowulf*. Robinson's argument, discussed in chapter 1, asserts that the appositive dyad—which characterizes the smallest elements of grammatical structure on through to the broadest thematic elements—resolves into a third entity, a "meaning" collocated by the reader and implied by the poet. To interpret the first two elements, a third comes into play; opposition, or apposition, is resolved or encompassed, a process adumbrated by Tolkien in his notion of "balance." The dynamics of opposition/apposition recast metonymic and metaphoric principles in terms of binarism, a principle of identifying and hierarchizing binary oppositions. In the next chapter I shall show how pieces of the poem have been occasionally contorted or distorted to comply with the logic of this binary mode, whose inherent demand for resolution and completion reflects another facet of the impulse to make parts into wholes.

In the previous chapter, I also suggested that we can resist this impulse, or replace it, by positing a nonteleological, nonhierarchical coexistence of the metaphoric and metonymic modes. The semiotic argument of this chapter offers a means of concretizing this abstract interpretational principle, a means of conceptualizing the process in which one and two are not inevitably three, nor must one be chosen over two, but one and two exist in a dynamic corelation. The notion of dyadic resolution, moreover, cannot address or encompass the dynamism of the poem as successfully as the concept of the triadic production of meaning, which, as we shall see, is central to Charles Sanders Peirce's theory of signs.

Putting aside the question of a possible overview, or final resolution of the poem's oppositional or appositional elements, in the reader's immediate engagement with the text such resolution is temporary, even mercurial. The narrative progression of the poem foils logical or linear attempts to sum up, to stand back and conclude that *this,* after all, meant *that.* The poem is essentially nonlinear, describing arcs and circles where persons, events, histories, and stories continually intersect. As I have emphasized in the Introduction, this poem requires a critical confrontation with difference. *Beowulf* is a text that invites a challenge to assumptions about the possibility and desirability of a structural overview. The quicksilver nature of its structure, where individual elements persist, dissolve, and expand in a continuum of resonance and association, questions the notion of textual boundaries as a form of resolution and suggests instead the infinitude of the text. To match the mode of the poem, it may be necessary to postulate and accept the text as without limit, to begin by "infinitizing the totality" (Kristeva, 1980: 175).

To allow the text to be infinite is to weave the web of *différance,* to "allow the different threads and lines of sense or force" to come together or separate freely; and it is a kind of permission that need not result in a sea of indeterminacy. In this chapter, I want to use two related approaches that help to image this process of weaving, and to construct a critical apparatus that can more specifically describe the operation of the web. Much of this chapter will be devoted to constructing this critical apparatus, and I shall take up implicit questions of textual infinitude, and of the reader's connection to it, explicitly in the final section. The first approach, that of visual analogy and interartistic comparison, will be familiar to Anglo-Saxonists; the second, a semiotic critical approach, is one that is just beginning to gain some recognition.

More organic critical approaches to *Beowulf,* which view its structure as cyclical and cumulative, and as an analogue of Anglo-Saxon art, have opened up far-reaching and fruitful areas of investigation into the nature of poetic structure.[2] The most pervasive characteristic of Anglo-Saxon art, found in all art forms from work in precious metal to manuscript illumination, is the use of interlace technique. The term refers to an intricate mode of decoration "having as its main characteristics the absence of any visual centre, luxuriant and coiling repetitions, an elusive patterning which defies attempts to perceive the whole design at once" (Shippey, 28). Interlace technique possesses an "inherent power of expansion. . . . Never at rest, it has an elasticity for expansion or contraction so that, like liquid in a container, it is able to adapt itself to the passages it must fill, if necessary changing shape from one design to the next" (Nordenfalk, 18–19). In a manner that recalls the immediate impact of the metonymic mode in language, interlace produces an experience—a dynamic, essentially kinetic, effect.

In his discussion of the interlace structure of *Beowulf*, John Leyerle argues that the interweaving of themes and motifs in the poem is a poetic structural analogue of interlace design, as elaborate, painstaking, and complex as the most sumptuous carpet page of an illuminated manuscript. Contemplation of the poem's design also provides an experience of its particular dynamic, and a reflexive examination of the contemplative exercise itself yields these insights: "This design reveals the meaning of coincidence, the recurrence of human behaviour, and the circularity of time, partly through the coincidence, recurrence, and circularity of the medium itself—the interlace structure" (Leyerle, 8).

Interlace as reflective of the poem's nonlinear progression also describes "an organizing principle closer to the workings of the human imagination proceeding in its atemporal way from one associative idea to the next than to the Aristotelian order of parts belonging to a temporal sequence with a beginning, middle and end" (Leyerle, 14), a view that both recalls and reiterates the argument of chapter 1 where the predominance of the metonymic mode of language allows a greater primacy and closeness to actual cognition.

Leyerle and other critics have done much in Old English criticism to help dissolve perceptual barriers, enabling us to see one cultural artistic sign, a design or a painting, in terms of another, a text. Critical objections to discussing poetry in artistic terms, most recently voiced by Morton Bloomfield in his analysis of the inadequacy of the term "interlace" to describe Old English poetry, are based on the premise that a text is unavoidably and inevitably *not* a painting. Bloomfield asserts that we can never break "the iron rule of narrative that two lines of action cannot be *presented to the reader or listener at the same time*" (52). The simultaneity possible in visual art has no parallel in verbal art, and hence the interlace analogy must always, to an extent, fail. A semiotic viewpoint, and especially that of Charles Sanders Peirce, attenuates this impasse. While my emphasis is less on the perspective of simultaneity than on the kinetic affinity of these visual and textual media, the important point here is that a semiotic perspective does not seek to identify one sign system with another but to look at how the systems connect with and inform each other. Jonathan Evans reminds medievalists of the value of an important basic principle of modern semiotics: "if culture is an array of signs or of sign-systems . . . then no semiotic phenomenon can be fully comprehended in an analytical theory that assumes discreteness between the various systems of signs in a culture" (1986: 129). Moreover, if we are prepared to accept that "the interartistic comparison inevitably reveals the aesthetic norms of the period" (Steiner, 18), we may learn a great deal about sign-functioning in the world evoked by the Old English poem by pursuing and extending the domain of the comparison.

In the following discussion I extend the domain of the artistic to include that of the artifact, and I talk about the sign-function of material objects—primarily swords—in *Beowulf*. It should be noted that most of the objects in *Beowulf*, and especially the swords, would have been, according to external and internal evidence, highly sophisticated works of art in their own right. The sword functions as many signs—physical, visual, and linguistic—within the poem: it is a gorgeous treasure prized for its beauty, a symbol of love or loyalty or shame, a reminder of the past, an incitement to future revenge, and much more. The sword signs are both inter- and extratextual, anchored within the narrative as linguistic signs, but evolving through their interrelationship and reverberating without and beyond the text. The nature of the interaction of linguistic signs in the poem mirrors the kinetic dynamic of interlace; it translates our relation to the text into a more visual, physical, material connection with it, one that possesses the immediacy of fact, feeling, or action. Examining how these kinds of sword signs cohere within the text can provide a means of describing the mercurial movement of the text in a manner that matches and retains the regenerative irresolution and visual infinitude of interlace. A semiotic approach also helps to explain one facet of this poem's extraordinary density and power.

The sign for "sword," it may be at once objected, must always be a linguistic one: that is, the Old English word for sword or one of the many descriptive epithets used in its place. And language must always be at one or several removes from reality and experience. Moreover, any good poem is larger than the sum of its signs; it will reverberate within our minds, possibly even change them, in an equally dynamic way. But the extended visual, material domain I am claiming for the linguistic sign in *Beowulf* will depend for its validation on a gradual process of semiotic analysis and reconstruction; it will require permission from the reader, a suspension of judgment, and a temporary dissolution of word/object boundaries, until I arrive at a consideration of how signs cohere in this text.

Peirce's Concept of Sign

Semiotic criticism is gradually gaining recognition from medievalists and there have been several attempts to incorporate sign theory in discussions of Old and Middle English literature.[3] Although there have been some specifically Peircean analyses of medieval texts,[4] the "semeiotic" (a spelling Peirce introduced and one that I will use when referring specifically to Peirce's theories), or philosophical, mathematical, and logical system of sign analysis of Charles Sanders Peirce often appears by implication only, these ideas having been so profoundly and pervasively influential that they now form the bases of general principles in modern semiotics. I want to return to Peirce's original hypotheses, and will use some of the formulas of Peirce's system because of their value in constructing a specific critical apparatus.

There are several compelling reasons to use Peirce's system of sign analysis; its comprehensiveness and flexibility make it especially appropriate to the kind of argument I am constructing about levels of cross-signification in *Beowulf.* Peirce's semeiotic encompasses far more than just language; we can interpret all experience in terms of semeiosis, as Peirce states in a well-known letter to Lady Welby: "It has never been in my power to study anything, — mathematics, ethics, metaphysics, gravitation, thermodynamics, optics, chemistry, comparative anatomy, astronomy, psychology, phonetics, economics, the history of science, whist, men and women, wine, metrology, except as a study of semeiotic" (Hardwick, 85–86).

Peirce defines the sign itself in very broad terms:

A sign, or *representamen*, is something which stands to somebody for something in some respect or capacity. (2.228)[5]

I define a Sign as anything which is so determined by something else, called its Object, and so determines an effect upon a person, which effect I call its Interpretant, that is the latter is mediately determined by the former. (Hardwick, 80–81)

The effect of the sign, or its interpretant, may itself be a sign that determines another interpretant. Semeiosis involves continual translation, growth, and expansion:

A sign is not a sign unless it translates itself into another sign in which it is more fully developed. (5.594)

. . . a sign is something by knowing which we know something more. (Hardwick, 31–32)

Also important to my argument is that Peirce's conception of sign, and his trichotomous divisions of sign categories, are fundamentally connected to his phenomenological categories. The analysis and interpretation of signs always imply a concurrent analysis and interpretation of experience, and of the process of cognition. When applied to a text Peirce's terminology is particularly useful in describing connections, not only within the text, but between words and things, between the language of the text and the subject's experience of the text.

The focus on expansion and continual movement in sign interaction is one important aspect of Peirce's sign theory that matches the mode of *Beowulf.* The connection to experience also distinguishes Peirce's system in that it accounts for a subject and includes a role for the interpreter of signs. One of the limitations of contemporary semiotic theory, according to Teresa de Lauretis and Kaja Silverman, is that it does not fully address the role of the subject and the operations of desire.[6] Peirce's system "greatly complicates the picture in which a signifier would immediately correspond to a signified" (de Lauretis, 1984: 172) by replacing a Saussurean dualism with the more complex notion of triadic sign production. Umberto Eco asks the question, "What is, in the semiotic framework, the place of the *acting subject* of every semiosic act?" (314). De Lauretis points out that his answer engages the producer of signs, "the subject of enunciation or of a speech act, not its addressee or receiver; not the reader but the speaker/writer" (168). Peirce engages the user of signs. The sign has an effect "upon a person": "it stands to somebody for something. . . . It addresses somebody, that is, it creates in the mind of that person an equivalent sign, or perhaps a more developed sign" (2.228).

I shall return to Peirce's conception of the role of the interpreter in the final section of this chapter; here I want to stress that Peirce's attention to the role of the subject in the signifying process distinguishes his semeiotic, and will be particularly valuable as a means of extending the chapter 1 discussion of the nature of the reader's engagement with the Old English poetic text.

The triadic production of signs takes place on many levels; Peirce's system divides and subdivides in ways that are too complex to enumerate here. I propose instead to establish some working definitions for my purposes and to refer the reader to the extensive research on Peirce for more detailed explication.[7] I shall be referring primarily to the phenomenological categories of Firstness, Secondness, and Thirdness, to his best-known sign trichotomy, that of icon, index, and symbol, and to the division of types of interpretants—a very small fraction of Peirce's total system. The phenomenological categories are especially important because they provide an overarching perspective on all semeiosis:

My view is that there are three modes of being. I hold that we can directly observe them in elements of whatever is at any time before the mind in any way. There are the being of positive qualitative possibility, the being of actual fact, and the being of law that will govern facts in the future. (1.23)

It seems, then, that the true categories of consciousness are: first, feeling, the consciousness which can be included with an instant of time, passive consciousness of quality, without recognition or analysis; second, consciousness of an interruption into the field of consciousness, sense of resistance, of an external fact, of another something; third, synthetic consciousness, binding time together, sense of learning, thought. (1.353)[8]

The categories of Firstness, Secondness, and Thirdness underpin Peirce's other triadic divisions, including the second trichotomy of signs, which describes the sign in relation to its object (icon, index, symbol) and the classes of interpretant (Immediate, Dynamic, Final). I have included a sample of Peirce's definitions of icon, index, and symbol in my notes.[9] Here I refer to Shapiro's useful and straightforward summary of these sign types: "the relation between sign and object may be one of iconic resemblance (such as a portrait and the person portrayed), of indexical contiguity and dynamic interaction (smoke and fire), or of symbolic law (a habit, such as an item of language)" (1983: 40).

The last set of definitions that will figure prominently in my discussion of *Beowulf* involves the interpretant, "the cognition produced in the mind" (1.372), the effect that the sign determines in the mind of the interpreter:

My Immediate Interpretant is implied in the fact that each sign must have its peculiar interpretability before it gets any Interpreter. My Dynamical Interpretant is that which is experienced in each act of interpretation and is different in each from that of any other; and the Final Interpretant is the one Interpretative result to which every Interpreter is destined to come if the Sign is sufficiently considered. The Immediate Interpretant is an abstraction, consisting in a Possibility. The Dynamical Interpretant is a single actual event. The Final Interpretant is that towards which the actual tends. (Hardwick, 111)

Throughout most of this discussion, my primary focus will be on the second element of these various triadic structures; I shall argue that in *Beowulf* we enter a world characterized largely by Secondness, by Dynamical Interpretants, where indexicality is the dominant mode of signification and the compulsion of the *hic et nunc* claims and engages the reader. By this I do not mean to imply that there is an absence of synthesis, characterized by Thirdness or symbolicity. Just as metonymy may predominate without precluding the presence of metaphor, so too may the compulsion and dynamism of Secondness predominate without excluding the reflective, synthesizing consciousness of Thirdness—an analogue for the metaphorizing reader who collocates and resolves meaning. The coexistent dynamic of Secondness and Thirdness, and of metonymy and metaphor, are both means of examining the nature and possibility and extent of resolution in this text. Silverman notes that the commutability of the signified revealed in Peirce's notion of the interpretant parallels Derrida's "freeplay" (38); both concepts image the web of *différance*, the process of weaving. Peirce's terminology, however, in addition to offering a means of questioning literal or thematic textual boundaries, also engages the role of the subject in that process of questioning.

Words, Things, and the Space Between

Within the text the sign for sword is a linguistic one—that is, the occurrence of a word. Strictly speaking according to Peirce's first trichotomy of signs describing signs in relation to themselves (qualisign, sinsign, legisign), a word is a legisign, a third, instantiated in a particular instance by a sinsign, a second. Words fit most easily into the first trichotomy, and things, like swords, fit into the second trichotomy of icon, index, and symbol. A word will not have the iconic or indexical presence of an object, visual or material; it is not a picture, a pointing finger, or a billow of smoke. Though words can quite comfortably be symbols (it is possible to conflate the trichotomies), they always lack a "feeling of presence," the difference insisted on by Steiner in her discussion of textual and visual affect (21). The closest linguistic analogy to the pointing finger would be a pronoun: "all words are legisigns, although the indexical relation predominates over the symbolic in deictic words such as pronouns" (Shapiro, 1983: 45). Peirce in one instance exemplifies an index in terms of the moods of speech: "Icons and indices assert nothing. If an icon could be interpreted by a sentence, that sentence must be in a 'potential mood,' that is, it would merely say 'Suppose a figure had three sides,' etc. Were an index so interpreted, the mood must be imperative, or exclamatory, as 'See there!' or 'Look out!'" (2.291).

It is precisely this imperative mode, this quality of fixing and riveting attention, that I claim for the sign-functioning of the sword and other objects in *Beowulf*, for the linguistic signs for these objects. This is not really unusual; words often develop extreme indexical properties depending on our level of familiarity with them, or the associations that develop over a period of time (for example, ice cream points to good, delicious; anchovy points to tasty or revolting, according to your point of view). Our relation to a word can determine its degree of symbolicity or indexicality.

The interwoven networks of indexical connotations surrounding the term "sword" in *Beowulf* are dense and complex; interpreting these networks, even tracing their outline, involves an effort, a shift in vision that is in tune with the poem. Again, the interartistic comparison helps the reader to do this; if we allow the text to work upon us in the manner of interlace design, we can more easily follow the interplay of linguistic signs; we can begin to trace the interwoven networks of association and experience their indexical connective force. As with any poem, we build as we read what Peirce calls "collateral experience" of the objects of signs. "The sign can only represent the object and tell about it. It cannot furnish acquaintance with or recognition of that object" (2.231). "It can only indicate [the object] and leave the interpreter to find out by collateral experience" (8.314), which is "previous acquaintance with what the sign denotes" (NE3: 842). We may understand the meaning of a word by simple differentiation within a language system, but its actual use is discovered and developed through collateral observation, or increased understanding of its context. The poem is the context for our collateral observation of sword signs, but this context might legitimately be expanded beyond the text.

So far I have been hovering (perhaps precariously) in a space between words and things. The swords, or other objects in the poem, are not, of course, present in front of our eyes to scan like a picture (I do not intend to become fully embroiled in controversy about temporal-spatial divisions in art and poetry), nor would they have been for an Old English reader, or audience of the poem. But we can assume that the familiarity with the sword sign and its visual and semantic connotations would have been far greater for the contemporaneous reader or listener. This familiarity, Caroline Brady suggests, was both esthetic and practical; the audience of *Beowulf* "knew also about their weapons, their strengths and weaknesses, but above all about their swords upon the quality of which their lives depended" (108–9). Much the same principle of reconstruction applies to our understanding of the historical and mythological allusions in the poem. We can piece together a broader context, to inform ourselves and come closer to that contemporary familiarity and recognition, and so build our collateral experience.

The following brief and necessarily partial reconstruction of "sword lore" might help to establish the connection between sign and object, between swords and beautiful objects and their relation to words.

Most of the surviving artifacts of outstanding artistic merit in this period are illuminated manuscripts, but these, art historian

C. R. Dodwell insists, were not what the Anglo-Saxons cared for most. In fact precisely because books were less valued did they survive the plundering and pillage of successive Viking invasions. More highly valued was work in precious metals, which better reflected the Anglo-Saxon "love of resplendence"; objects like jeweled drinking cups, neck- and arm-rings of twisted gold, gold-filigreed helmets and wargear, the damascened blades and decorated hilts of swords—the clank and gleam of which pervade *Beowulf*. There is ample evidence that the poetic descriptions of these objects easily matched the reality: "the poets were not dreaming up gilded visions but delineating the tastes of the world around [them]" (Dodwell, 30). The love of resplendence is everywhere reflected. Evidence of Anglo-Saxon wills shows that swords were usually decorated with gold, as were spurs, musical instruments, and ships' prows.[10]

"In any unsettled society art treasures never lose their connotation of accessible wealth" (Dodwell, 25), and the material worth of these objects is often emphasized in the poetry. The minstrel in *Widsith*, Dodwell points out, knows the precise value of Eormanric's gift of an arm-ring (24). That treasures were relished and enjoyed as well forming a kind of currency is especially evident in *Beowulf*. John D. Niles calls attention to this parallel investiture of functional and esthetic significance: "In his sermon, Hrothgar could have made much of the vanity of earthly goods. Instead, he stresses the danger of a king's bottling up wealth. Rather than exhort his audience to forego material goods, time and again the poet dwells lovingly on the beauty or value of precious objects and speaks of the honor they lend their possessors" (223).

Elsewhere the poet lists and describes with care just how many treasures and of what kind Beowulf receives as payment or reward for his services. As Niles points out, the treasures comprise a moral, emotional currency as well: they express the sentiments of the giver, and transmit honor to the receiver. They approve Beowulf's actions and complement his courage.[11] The drinking cup acquires meaning in its ritual of passing from one warrior to another. Treasure acquires significance through its distribution.[12] This central part of the heroic ethos is reflected in the poem's vocabulary: the lord is *goldwine gumena* (gold-friend to men, 1602), a *beag-gyfa* (ring-giver, 1102), who distributes treasure in a *goldsele* (gold hall, 715).

Precious objects were often invested with human significance; this is seen not only in the pervasive use of personification in *Beowulf* but is well attested outside the context of the poem, and is especially true of swords: "Germanic and Old English poetic convention as well as Anglo-Saxon laws and beliefs encouraged the belief that a sword metonymically inherited and participated in the qualities, attainments, excellences as well as defects of its original owner and transmitted these almost magically to its wielder" (Viswanathan, 360). The sword might even substitute for its owner. In the Sutton Hoo burial no body was found;[13] the placement of grave goods, however, suggests that the sword was laid in its place (Bruce-Mitford, 53).

The esthetic and nonesthetic values of the object are closely linked; the more carefully decorated and ornate are his sword hilt and blade, the better the warrior. M. D. Cherniss points out that Anglo-Saxon warriors would not have worn campaign ribbons or medals, but would acquire increasingly more valuable (more highly decorated) war gear (1973: 245). The sword of good quality, one with a low carbon content to make it steely and flexible, would be judged according to the complexity and delicacy of its decorative pattern (Davidson, 21–23). The blade pattern was produced by damascening or pattern-welding, a painstaking process of welding strips of iron and wires together technically outlined by H. E. Davidson; the effect, however, is best described in her translation of Cassiodorus's fifth-century letter sent to thank another ruler for the present of several swords: "So resplendent is their polished clarity that they reflect with faithful distinctness the faces of those who look upon them. So evenly do their edges run down to a point that they might be thought not shaped by files but moulded by the furnace. The central part of their blades, cunningly hollowed out, appears to be grained with tiny snakes, and here such varied shadows play that you would believe the shining metal to be interwoven with colours" (106). Many of the swords in *Beowulf* are similarly designed. The use of *mæl* in compounds is a likely reference to pattern-welded blades, as in *brogdenmæl* (ornamented with a wavy pattern, 1667), *sceadenmæl* (branch-patterned, 1939) and *hringmæl* (ring-marked, 2037).[14]

The sword hilt would have been even more elaborately decorated, often displaying serpentine interlace motifs and occasionally inscribed with runes (as is the case with the giant sword in *Beowulf*), thereby intensifying its talismanic significance. The hilt of a king's sword also had special significance, forming part of a ceremony where retainers would pledge their allegiance. Historical evidence shows that the sword was an important heirloom, passed on from one generation to another, given, in some cases at birth along with a name, or later as a token of manhood (Davidson, 211–12). The "sword lore" of this period is extensive and makes for a fascinating study in its own right, but I shall finish this general reconstruction at this point and rely on the poem to extend and support it. Brady's comprehensive study has amply demonstrated that the poem is a mine of specific and practical information about weaponry in general, and swords in particular. A. T. Hatto's earlier study draws attention to the "niceties of sword lore, which the poet is so careful to observe" (148), and Davidson also believes that the *Beowulf* poet may be trusted for his accuracy: his descriptions of swords "imply considerable detailed knowledge of swords and their appearance" (147).

A sense of what the poem's objects look like and connote should provide some support for my occupation of the space between words and things, and examining the extent of the concept of personification offers a further means of demarcating this space. In a discussion of the ubiquitous device of personification in *Beowulf*, N. D. Isaacs suggests that each object possesses "a living, moving spirit of its own" (216). The sword may metonymically share human attributes, or the sword or other war gear may replace the warrior: when Beowulf and his men first arrive on the shores of Denmark, the suspicious coastguard sees not men approaching, but *beorhte randas* (bright shields, 231), or—a more important substitution—in the dragon fight, it is the sword that fails, and not Beowulf's strength.[15] Swords can also sing grim battle songs.[16] The notion of interchangeability of objects and persons also extends to words and deeds. The hero's words, or boast, must be tantamount to deeds; deeds, in turn, are equated with treasures as reward; deeds of the past are embodied by objects in the present; the appearance of an object in the present may incite future action.[17] And so we might go round in circles. Like the moving, intersecting spirals of interlace, it is not possible to think of all these exchanges and associations at once.

We cannot simply exchange or simultaneously identify sign systems; words are not deeds, and poems are not paintings, but we can look at the ways that these systems intersect. The poem is a continuum, an echo chamber, where we experience a continual crisscrossing of temporal-spatial values and relations, where the physical world subsumes the mental and vice versa, and where the linguistic sign develops its peculiar palpability, resonance, and kinetic power.

I note here another theoretical framework that provides a context for this notion of the palpability of the linguistic sign (or viscerality, in terms of the chapter 1 discussion of reader-response), one that will be important to the argument of the next chapter. I mention it briefly, to begin to establish a bridge from sign to gender, and to outline some further dimensions of the present discussion. The sign, especially the object sign, in *Beowulf* participates to some extent in the power of the primitive sign, as this is designated by Gilles Deleuze and Felix Guattari in their historicized account of the development of representation. In a text such as *Beowulf*, which embodies several coexistent cultural descriptions (oral and literate, pagan and Christian, "barbaric" and civilized society), the cultural and political context of sign development helps to further describe the nature of the sign-object relation and to demarcate words, things, and the space between.

In Deleuze and Guattari's formulation, there are two orders of "graphism," or inscription, which roughly correspond to barbarian and imperial modes of representation. In the barbarian, primitive system of representation, the sign is associated with physical territorial reality, and the violence and cruelty of the "inscription in the flesh";[18] it retains a vital, interactive, but unsubordinated connection with voice: "primitive societies are oral not because they lack a graphic system but because, on the contrary, the graphic system in these societies is independent of the voice; it marks signs on the body that respond to the voice, react to the voice, but that are autonomous and do not align themselves to it" (Deleuze and Guattari, 202). As the state develops and imposes "imperial" representation, this autonomy disappears; in the second order of graphism (a term that encompasses all systems of representation, legislative, bureaucratic, financial), writing supplants the voice by becoming subordinate to it, and makes way for arbitration, control, and resolution: "the voice no longer sings but dictates, decrees; the graphy no longer dances, it ceases to animate bodies, but is set into writing on tablets, stones, and books; the eye sets itself to reading" (205).

The first order of graphism or representation involves the visceral immediacy and self-referentiality allied with the metonymic mode. The primitive sign is "self-validating; it is a position of desire in a state of multiple connections. It is not a sign of a sign or a desire of a desire. It knows nothing of linear subordination . . . it is rhythm and not form, zig-zag and not line, artifact and not idea, production and not expression" (Deleuze and Guattari, 202).

Both sign orders coexist in *Beowulf*; in chapter 3 I shall look at words and deeds, at language and violence, as systems of representation. Here I want to point out that the concept of primitive sign also returns us to an emphasis on process and experience, and to a construction of interpretation *as* desire, whereas the "imperial" sign mirrors the symbolic metaphorizing function. As the metonym functions within, and also is a function of, the metonymic fabric of the whole text, so the sign in *Beowulf* accrues its visceral and primitive power in dynamic association, in a series of interwoven networks, verbal sign patterns that follow the twists, turns, and recursions of interlace.

The Web of Signs

Using Peirce's terminology, I will trace a partial outline of the poem's indexically connected networks, limiting my discussion to four representative strands of interrelation.[19] The first two strands involve cups and rings, the second two focus on swords. In unraveling separate strands of the poem in this fashion one could just as easily start at the end or the middle and work backward, but I shall initially adopt the arbitrary clarity of linear progression.

Beowulf has arrived at Hrothgar's court, has offered his assistance and made his heroic boast; he has inspired a measure of confidence and cheered the beleaguered Danish court to the point where a celebratory feast takes place. Hrothgar takes up the narrative; he recalls the recent past in which his own retainers drank and boasted over their ale-cups that they could defeat Grendel. After a gruesome description of their failure (mead hall and benches dripping with blood, 484–87), Hrothgar exhorts Beowulf to enjoy the present feast. This is ceremonially affirmed by a servant who circulates around the company pouring the shining drink (*scir wered*, 496) from a decorated ale-cup (*hroden ealowæge*, 495). Following Unferth's hostile challenge to Beowulf—

which undercuts the image of hall unity implicit in ale-sharing—
Wealhtheow introduces a more festive note when she appears
with a ritual drinking cup, and passes it around. The gold-
adorned queen offers the precious vessel (*sincfato*, 622) to
Beowulf. The cup next appears in the narrative after Beowulf has
fought Grendel, and there is a great celebration in Heorot where
Hrothgar and his nephew Hrothulf feast together and share
medoful manig (many a mead-cup, 1915).

There follows the extremely sobering tale of Finn and Hengest,
and of Hildeburh, the "peace-weaving" woman caught in the
middle of their enmity, which is recounted as entertainment by
Hrothgar's court poet. Gold-adorned Wealhtheow brings forth
another ceremonial drinking cup and makes a speech that is a
remarkable mixture of ceremonial affirmation of peace and unity,
justifiable political paranoia, and controlled desperation. In an
attempt to look out for her two sons, she issues a public re-
minder/admonition to her husband who has acted rather rashly in
offering to adopt Beowulf as his son when he already has two of
his own. Her speech also encourages the now proven hero to
declare his support for her sons in front of Hrothulf, the poten-
tially treacherous nephew who might usurp the Danish throne
before her sons come of age. (Wealhtheow's situation might also
recall the position of the hapless "peace-weaver" Hildeburh, the
wife of Finn.)[20] She carries the cup to Beowulf and gives him more
precious objects. But thereby hangs another thread.

Let me stop here and gather up this thread so far. These several
drinking cups are not important or famous in themselves; they do
not have names or histories, but these objects denote and develop
a series of indexically connected associations. The different lin-
guistic signs for cup are indexical sinsigns that compel attention
to the object and determine a series of dynamic interpretants that
are in turn indexical signs. A kind of chain reaction is set up. The
indexical connections can be traced more clearly by means of
diagrams, although in the diagrams that follow one point should
be emphasized. The broken arrow lines connecting the triangles
should be understood as indicating accumulation rather than
contingency; that is, the sign accrues meanings, so that each
successive triangle incorporates the preceding ones and thus
represents a varied accumulation of meanings.

Figure 1 shows how the linguistic signs grow and develop each
time they are interpreted; the text provides an overall network

Figure 1

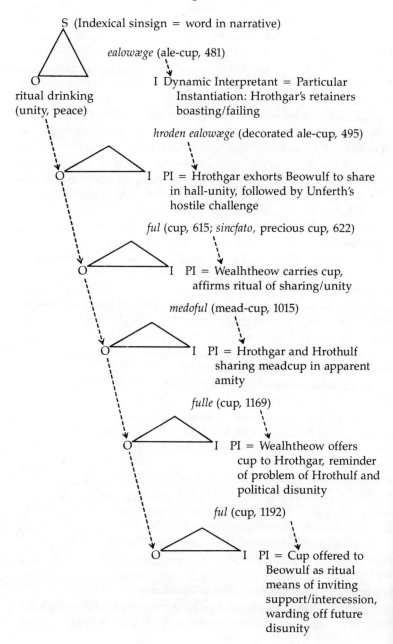

S (Indexical sinsign = word in narrative)

ealowæge (ale-cup, 481)

O
ritual drinking
(unity, peace)

I Dynamic Interpretant = Particular
Instantiation: Hrothgar's retainers
boasting/failing

hroden ealowæge (decorated ale-cup, 495)

O ————————I PI = Hrothgar exhorts Beowulf to share
in hall-unity, followed by Unferth's
hostile challenge

ful (cup, 615; *sincfato*, precious cup, 622)

O ————————I PI = Wealhtheow carries cup,
affirms ritual of sharing/unity

medoful (mead-cup, 1015)

O ————————I PI = Hrothgar and Hrothulf
sharing meadcup in apparent
amity

fulle (cup, 1169)

O ————————I PI = Wealhtheow offers
cup to Hrothgar, reminder
of problem of Hrothulf and
political disunity

ful (cup, 1192)

O ————————I PI = Cup offered to
Beowulf as ritual
means of inviting
support/intercession,
warding off future
disunity

wherein each interpretation (a dynamic interpretant, which re-
ceives a particular instantiation in the text) becomes another
index, dynamically, inevitably pointing to its interpretant. Each
time the sign appears in the narrative, it may trigger this succes-
sion and become part of a chain reaction.

The linguistic sign for the object accumulates an indexical
presence parallel to more obvious or literal narrative indices in the
poem, like Grendel's claw nailed to the entrance of Heorot as a
victory advertisement, and the inevitable sequel, the head of
Aeschere, Hrothgar's beloved advisor, displayed on the path to the
mere—an index to both Grendel's mother's past revenge and to
Beowulf's future retaliation. Or the sword placed on Hengest's
lap, which triggers his retaliation against Finn; and the ancestral
sword of the Heathobards worn by a young warrior, the simple
sight of which starts a fight in memory of the history of its
acquisition.

Taking up another strand in the poem, one can trace a similar
sign function for objects with a specific history evoked by the
narrative. As Wealhtheow approaches Beowulf with the ritual
drinking cup, she also rewards him with treasures:

> Him wæs ful boren,   ond freondlaþu
> wordum bewægned,   ond wunden gold
> estum geawed,   earmhreade twa,
> hrægl ond hringas,   healsbeaga mæst
> þara þe ic on foldan   gefrægen hæbbe.   (1192–96)

(The cup was carried to him, and friendship offered with words,
and twisted gold bestowed with good will, two arm-ornaments, a
corselet and rings, the greatest neck-ring that I ever heard tell of.)

The poet, however, *does* know of another, even greater, such
treasure, and singles out the neck-ring for further comment. It
was matched in the past by the legendary Brosings' necklace,
acquired amid feuding, treachery, and death. Moving back into
the present, the poet forecasts the future of Beowulf's gift: it will
be worn by Hygelac (to whom Beowulf, loyal retainer that he is,
will turn over all acquired treasures upon his return home) on a
reckless raid in which he will die, and the treasure will fall to
wyrsan wigfrecan (worse warriors, 1212), the Franks. Back in the
present in the narrative, Wealhtheow exhorts Beowulf to enjoy
his treasure ("*Bruc disses beages*," 1216). This sequence is illustrated
in figure 2. Note also in this sequence how cup and ring linguistic

signs/indexes intersect beautifully when Hygelac carries the precious treasure on his raid *ofer yða ful* (over the cup of the waves, 1208).

The irony in the Figure 2 sequence is palpable; the gorgeous neck-ring weighs like a millstone on the narrative, but the ornament also fixes a continuum, where past, future, and present reflect, imply, and indexically connect with each other. Niles argues that the complex sense of time in *Beowulf* is one of its most distinguishing elements and adds another dimension to the possibilities for sign interaction; the poem crisscrosses both literal and imaginary time zones:

Mythic time, legendary time and historical time are all present
simultanaeously *in potentia* from the beginning of the poem to the end.
At any moment, as a way of making the involutions of the text more
dense, the poet may allude to persons or actions that pertain to any
of these three modes of time. Thus a given moment is not exactly a
narrative event, for nothing much may happen in it to advance the plot.
It is rather a kind of narrative "crossroads" for the intersection of lines
drawn from significant points in and out of time. (1983: 195)

I am also suggesting that this kind of "crossroads" can occur at the level of the linguistic sign for objects, whichever time zone we enter. During the dragon fight Wiglaf's sword acquires a similar repercussive density, functioning also as a narrative index, in that the poet breaks off in the middle of the fight to talk about the sword.[21] The result is an expansion of the simultaneity of perspective, which can also operate at the phraseological level; in chapter 1 we saw how the metonymical juxtaposition of time frames in several lines from *Daniel* aligns past and present in layered, contiguous association. In *Beowulf* the indexical sword sign holds past, present, and future perspectives before us in a process of inevitable and dynamic coalition. Without further paraphrase, Figure 3 should illustrate this series of connections.

In interpreting these sword signs, which engage a temporal perspective, an important question arises: To what extent are we "binding time together," moving from the dynamism of Secondness into the reflective synthesis of Thirdness? This is a question that I must partially address before examining the fourth, most complex sword sequence in the poem. I have emphasized the indexical quality of the object signs in the poem and therefore the quality of Secondness, "found in action, resistance, facticity,

Figure 2

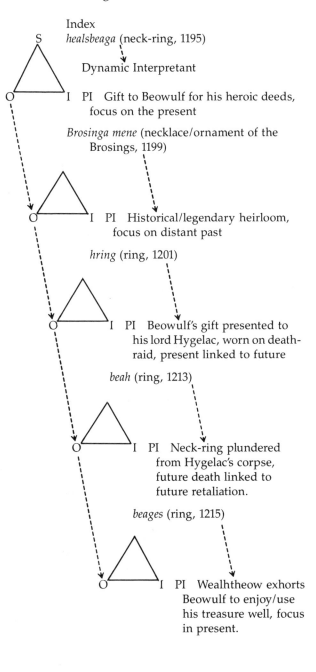

Index
healsbeaga (neck-ring, 1195)

S

Dynamic Interpretant

O   I   PI   Gift to Beowulf for his heroic deeds,
focus on the present

treasure
reward/gift

Brosinga mene (necklace/ornament of the
Brosings, 1199)

O   I   PI   Historical/legendary heirloom,
focus on distant past

hring (ring, 1201)

O   I   PI   Beowulf's gift presented to
his lord Hygelac, worn on death-
raid, present linked to future

beah (ring, 1213)

O   I   PI   Neck-ring plundered
from Hygelac's corpse,
future death linked to
future retaliation.

beages (ring, 1215)

O   I   PI   Wealhtheow exhorts
Beowulf to enjoy/use
his treasure well, focus
in present.

Figure 3

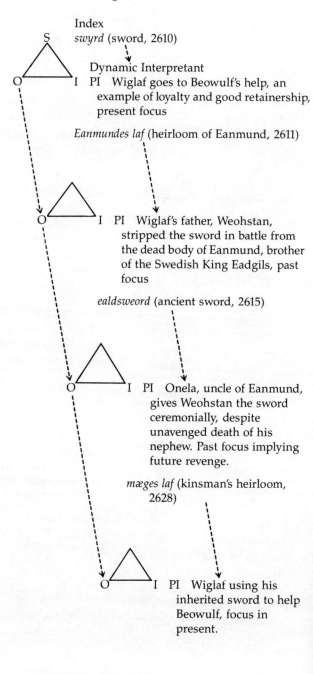

Index
swyrd (sword, 2610)

Dynamic Interpretant

S

O — I PI   Wiglaf goes to Beowulf's help, an example of loyalty and good retainership, present focus

fight

Eanmundes laf (heirloom of Eanmund, 2611)

O — I PI   Wiglaf's father, Weohstan, stripped the sword in battle from the dead body of Eanmund, brother of the Swedish King Eadgils, past focus

ealdsweord (ancient sword, 2615)

O — I PI   Onela, uncle of Eanmund, gives Weohstan the sword ceremonially, despite unavenged death of his nephew. Past focus implying future revenge.

mæges laf (kinsman's heirloom, 2628)

O — I PI   Wiglaf using his inherited sword to help Beowulf, focus in present.

dependence, relation, compulsion, effect, reality, and result" (Shapiro, 1983: 30). Shapiro's list in many ways provides an accurate general characterization of the world of the poem. The action-packed, dynamic aspect of the narrative is part of its resonance and power. It is not surprising that the popularity and appeal of *Beowulf* persists in, and translates easily into, comic-book form. In this regard, it is important to remember that Peirce differentiated two kinds of index, exemplified by demonstrative and relative pronouns:

> While demonstrative and personal pronouns are, as ordinarily used, "genuine indices," relative pronouns are "degenerate indices"; for though they may, accidentally and indirectly, refer to existing things, they directly refer, and need only refer, to the images in the mind which previous words have created. (2.305)

> If the Secondness is an existential relation, the Index is *genuine.* If the secondness is a reference, the Index is degenerate. (2.274)

The difference might be simply stated as having something pointed out to you initially, or being reminded rather insistently that it is already there. Broadly speaking, we could parallel these two kinds of connections to the difference between modern and medieval standards and definitions of artistry. The genuine index is more prized in the modern view; creative artistry lies in the surprise and innovation of connection, in the breaking up and remaking of possibly complacent patterns of habitual association. In the world of *Beowulf,* however, the power and effect of the index accumulate through the very inevitability of connection, the very predictability of reference. Using conventional poetic diction and formulas, the Old English poet might not appear to be a maker or remaker of language and hence perception, but a reshaper, a reemphasizer of familiar experience using familiar language. This means that we pay ever closer attention to the same things — honor, shame, feuds, loyalty, decision making, sorrow, loss and, above all, death — a relentlessness of focus that is discussed at length in chapter 3. Instead of enlargement or expansion, the process is one of increasingly minute and inescapable focus.

The psychological action of the index, Peirce says, does not depend "upon intellectual operations" (2.305). To what extent, then, is the poem locked into a world of Secondness, a world devoid of synthesis and reflection, or of interpretation in the hermeneutic sense? What is the place of Firstness and Thirdness, of icons and symbols? Is the poem a series of dynamic interpretants that never become, or even point toward, a Final interpretant? The simple repetitive operation of dynamic interpretants can stop semeiosis, the continual translation and expansion of signs:

> Dynamic interpretants, being finite bounded events, bring semeiosis to a terminus. A simple additive sequence of actions without cumulation into a pattern of habit remains, according to Peirce, at the level of dead Secondness. It is powerless to register the significance of a sign, or to be the sign of some object by signifying yet another sign of the same object. For this reason, Peirce concludes, there must be principles, norms, and laws that guide the interpretation of signs beyond the endless mechanical repetition of identical patterns of behavior. (Shapiro, 1983: 55–56)

It should be obvious at this point that I think that the Secondness of *Beowulf* is far from "dead." The lines of indexically connected triangles I have been tracing may eventually connect and become a circle. What Lewis Nicholson says of themes and motifs is also true of signs in the poem: "Just as the spirals of Anglo-Saxon ornament move forward to form intricate patterns and then return to themselves uninterrupted, so one may compare the intricacies of the poetic text where a theme or motif returns to itself like a snake with its tail in its mouth" (Nicholson, 1980: 245–46). The drinking cup resurfaces at the end of the poem as the provocation of the dragon's wrath. An unhappy exiled slave steals it from the dragon's hoard as a peace offering to his lord; the gesture toward reconciliation arouses the hatred and vengeance of the sleeping dragon.

Another cup gleams in the pile of treasures next to the dragon's dead body (3047–48), and might easily be one of the many treasures of twisted gold that are burnt on Beowulf's funeral pyre; which funeral might justifiably, if not indexically, recall that of Scyld Scefing at the beginning of the poem—a king's body pushed out to sea surrounded by a pile of gleaming treasures (36–40). Or the *earmbeaga fela / searwum gesæled* (many arm-rings cleverly twisted, 2763–64) that Beowulf stares at (some have said greedily) when he first surveys the dragon's magnificent hoard connect in our minds with the gifts Beowulf leaves to Wiglaf as he dies:

> Dyde him of healse   hring gyldenne
> þioden þristhydig,   þegne gesealde
> geongum garwigan,   goldfahne helm,
> beah ond byrnan,   het hyne brucan well.   (2809–12)

(The bold-minded king took from his neck the golden ring, and gave
to the thane, young spear-warrior, gold-adorned helmet, collar and
corselet, bade him use them well.

We cannot help recall Wealhtheow's ill-fated gift and her words
to the young Beowulf earlier in the poem. And so the signs of the
poem indexically connect and form intersecting circles. But these
are not the vicious and entrapping circles of "dead" Secondness;
like the recursions of interlace, they gather and spiral in a process
of inherent expansion.

The Giant Sword Hilt: A Path out of Secondness

The last sign-sequence, or thread, that I will trace through the
poem provides an especially appropriate forum for some recur-
rent questions and also returns the discussion to the role of the
subject, or interpreter of signs. To ask how or if we move from the
dynamic indexicality of Secondness to the synthesizing symbol-
icity of Thirdness is to raise questions of teleology once more: To
what extent is there resolution of meaning in the poem, or is the
text infinite? And how is the reading subject involved in either the
marking out or dissolution of textual boundaries?

To frame answers to these questions I turn to Peirce's views on
teleology and the subject as a context for the analysis of the final
sequence. Semeiosis is a teleologically motivated process for
Peirce, but he places considerable emphasis on the aspect of
process. A sign may determine any number of dynamic interpre-
tants, but possesses only one final interpretant; this is arrived at
through "sufficient consideration" of the sign, but it does not need
to be actualized in order to exist as a potential goal—"a being *in
futuro* will suffice" (2.92). For Peirce, the process of sufficient
consideration is itself teleological:

The idea of a final interpretant presupposes that of a goal of
interpretation. For apart from such a goal, "consideration" of a sign
would not lead the interpreter to any "destined" conclusion: regardless
of the amount of consideration made, any conclusion would remain
just as good. But if each sign has a unique final interpretant, then each
sign is the sign that it is in relation not only to a ground but also to
a goal of interpretation. It is clear, then, that Peirce conceived of
semeiosis as a teleological process and of signs as being what their
potential role in semeiosis makes them to be. (Short, 214)

If, as Short suggests, signs are what their role in semeiosis makes them to be, then the process of sign interaction itself—the progress toward the Final interpretant—is an important factor in the construction of meaning. And the user or interpreter of signs as a part of the process of triadic sign interaction is also implicated in the construction of meaning. The "meaning" of a sign, its interpretant, is a "cognition produced in the mind," which is yet another sign, but "perhaps a more developed one." Semeiosis, in both text and reader, is an ongoing and reciprocal process, one that engages self and text, inner and outer worlds (de Lauretis, 1987: 40). The importance of process is well described in the concept of Thirdness: "By the third, I mean the medium or connecting bond between the absolute first and last. The beginning is first, the end second, the middle third. . . . Continuity represents Thirdness almost to perfection. Every process comes under that head. . . . The positive degree of an adjective is first, the superlative second, the comparative third" (1.337).

In this view teleology is a function of continual translation. Peirce adds a new dimension here to the metonymic/metaphoric framework of chapter 1; his concept of Thirdness overcomes the closure of metaphoricity and describes a dynamic relational coexistence of the two modes, and, moreover, this is a dynamic in which the reader thoroughly participates. If we are "spoken" by the metonymic text, or claimed by the compulsion of Secondness, it is with a permission that itself represents the mediating presence of Thirdness. Our permission is here an acknowledgment of and a participation in semeiosis as process.

In Peirce's view, the self is also in process, continually in production as a user and producer of signs; it is, itself, a sign, a point I shall return to at the conclusion of this chapter. Subjectivity is an ongoing construction, and halting semeiosis or deciding on final meaning may itself only be a function of what Peirce calls habit, or what de Lauretis redefines as "experience . . . a complex of habits resulting from the semiotic interaction of 'outer world' and 'inner world,' the continuous engagement of a self or subject in social reality" (1984: 182). The reader who is collocating meaning, achieving the overview of metaphoricity, must beware the trap of Secondness, the lure of the superlative. "In the hierarchy of signs relative to their final interpretants, the highest or ultimate purpose is reached in the dominance of critical control over habits and beliefs" (Shapiro, 1983: 58). The interpreter of signs must continually reassess the habit of interpretation: meaning, or a truly "living definition," can be created only by "the deliberately formed, self-analyzing habit—self-analyzing because formed by the aid of analysis of the exercises that nourished it" (5.491).

Although Peirce insists on the goal-directed nature of all semeiosis, the potential for hermeneutic circularity and subjectivity in interpreting poetic signs is attenuated in several ways.[22] The interpreter's awareness and self-questioning matches the ever-developing, teleological determinacy of the sign under interpretation, suggesting an isomorphic developmental relation between reader and text. Signs become clearer: "the symbol is essentially a purpose," writes Peirce, "that is, a representation that seeks to make itself definite, or seeks to produce an interpretant more definite than itself" (NE4.261). As Ricoeur points out in his reevaluation of the hermeneutic circle,[23] the process or result of interpretation need not reflect merely circular reasoning or understanding; teleology in Peirce's system may be understood not in terms of circularity, but rather, in Shapiro's view, "it is more precisely a *spiral,* consisting of organically successive complementary links" (1983: 10). Shapiro's terminology describes the conjunctive development of reader and text in semeiosis, while it also recalls the expansive coils of interlace and the connecting triangles of object signs, both means of imaging the semiotic construction of meaning in *Beowulf.*

I conclude this brief overview of Peirce's thinking on teleology and subjectivity, and return to the poem, approaching this final sign-sequence with several Peircean questions in mind. To what extent, for example, does the increasing determinacy of the signs of the poem define a path out of Secondness? The very insistence of Secondness, the networks of reinforcements of a particular mode, might in themselves point to Thirdness. In his study of interlace in *Beowulf,* Nicholson concludes that the recurrence inherent in the interlace technique, while it may not provide directionality, may still be an insistent and subtle way of raising "the great questions of the poem" (250). How far does the sign interaction of the text itself go toward shaping those questions, or defining a path out of Secondness, and how does the reader also shape and discover this path?

I have argued that the dynamic, indexical mode of sign interaction predominates in *Beowulf,* but that this predominance by no means precludes the possibility of the synthesizing force of Thirdness. The signs of the poem achieve such synthesis par excellence on occasion; although, as we shall see, the continual translation of signs precludes stasis or resolution—a Final interpretant remains *in futuro*—Hrothgar's so-called sermon is a remarkable and multifaceted prism of sign interaction. Beowulf has defeated Grendel and his mother, and is about to return home; Hrothgar warns the young hero of the dangers of pride and reminds him of his own mortality. The "sermon" is inspired as Hrothgar gazes on the hilt of the giant sword from Grendel's cave (the blade has dissolved in the poisonous blood of the monsters). This, and Grendel's head—another powerfully literal index in the poem—were the only "treasures" that Beowulf carried home as spoils.

At this point in the narrative, the sword hilt may be seen as several signs—icon, index, and symbol. It is a gorgeous, gleaming esthetic object, one of the many objects in the poem whose visual and physical presence is strongly evoked. The iconicity, the quality of Firstness, of precious objects emerges as a result of the rich vocabulary attached to them, the many epithets and descriptive compounds that often extract and focus on a single quality, a gleam, or pattern. A sword may be a *beaduleoma* (battlelight, 1523) as it flashes in battle; it may be *brunecg* (brown-edged, 1546) or *grægmæl* (gray-colored/marked, 2682) according to the bronze or silvery metallic cast of the gleam of its blade; it may be *swate fah* (stained/colored with blood, 1286) or *since fage* (adorned with treasure/jewels, 1615). The icon, or image, can flicker and change, like the cross in the *Dream of the Rood*, as the poet exploits the several meanings and forms of *fag/fah* (colored, stained, decorated, variegated). He describes Hrunting, the sword given to Beowulf by an apparently repentant Unferth, as *atertanum fah* (gleaming/stained with venom-twigs, 1459), an "excellent kenning for serpents," Davidson suggests, and an "imaginative way of describing the serpentine patterns on the blade which caught the fancy of Cassiodorus long before" (130). The metonymic quality and context of the descriptive compound discussed in chapter 1 also contributes to the visual presence, the present impact of the object's iconicity, the evocation and intimation (which cannot be actualized) of the idea of pure quality and feeling that is Firstness. The gorgeous hilt of the giant sword gleams within, reflects, the narrative:

> Swa wæs on ðæm scennum   sciran goldes
> þurh runstafas   rihte gemearcod,

geseted ond gesæd,   hwam þæt sweord geworht,
irena cyst   ærest wære,
wreoþenhilt   ond wyrmfah.   (1694–98)

(On the sword-guards of shining gold it was rightly marked out in
rune-staves, set down and told, for whom that sword, best of irons,
was first made, with twisted hilt and serpentine markings.)

In a narrative and thematic context, the giant sword hilt is one
of the most significant objects in the poem, and its iconicity is
comprehensive. Lewis Nicholson points out that the description
of the artifact in some instances "suggests the texture of the
poetry itself" (1975: 57) and this is certainly true of this highly
sophisticated icon, a kind of portrait of the poem. It functions in
much the same way as a diagram, or an algebraic equation that
"*exhibits* . . . the relations of the quantities concerned" (2.274),
which are the visual and textual (narrative) structure. The hilt
could be seen as an icon of the text, which Hrothgar takes up as *the
text* for his sermon, and which he then *reads* and *interprets* within
the text.

This remarkable prism of sign interaction and apparent synthe-
sis has even more facets. Is Hrothgar actually *reading* the sword as
text, or is he making it his own text, or are we as readers claiming
it as our text? James W. Earl argues that the appearance of the
magical giant sword hilt and Hrothgar's "reading" of it represent
one of the "few clearly symbolic portions of the narrative" that the
poet explicates for us (1979: 81). It "announces its own role in the
poem . . . it is an iconographic commentary upon the destruction
of the race of Grendel, which Beowulf has just accomplished" (84).

Allen J. Frantzen, on the other hand, calls attention to the fact
that the story on the hilt is one of beginnings, not endings: "the
hilt does not depict the end of the race of Cain, but rather the flood
that unsuccessfully tried to end that race" (1990). One of the main
purposes of Frantzen's thought-provoking argument is to show
how the story on the hilt is actually a textual *aporia*, one of the
poem's many gaps and puzzles, one of the several untold stories
in the poem awaiting telling, and one that tempts the reader to
take over and finish the poet's task.

From the point of view of sign interaction, however, let me first
postulate that when Hrothgar "interprets" the sword hilt the icon
becomes translated into a symbol. We can read the sermon as an
assemblage of many of the possible dynamic interpretants of the

sword signs; the hilt is an epitomizing, encapsulating icon, while it also seems to clear a pathway through and out of the grip of Secondness into Thirdness.

The hilt initially retains, like so many of the other objects in the poem, a powerful indexical function: not only do the rune staves "spell out" the origin and history of ancient strife (*fyrngewinnes*, 1689), the presence of the hilt operates as Hrothgar's cue to speak. But Hrothgar interrupts the indexical pointer to combat, breaks the chain reaction and makes the hilt itself an object; his speech is an associative, connecting flow of dynamic interpretants over which Hrothgar apparently assumes control because he allows, in fact insists upon, the symbolicity of the object. Again, a diagram (see Figure 4) may be a clearer way to describe how the speech works from a semeiotic standpoint, although my rough paraphrases of this powerful speech should be understood as merely functional, shortcut references to one of the most complex and debated passages in the poem.

Returning to the issues of teleology, of directions and goals, and of the reader's contribution to constructing meaning, I am left with more questions and the emerging presence of paradox—the subject of the next chapter. Perhaps all Hrothgar has done in his famous sermon is to contribute his own collateral experience to our ongoing interpretation of the sword signs in the poem. Perhaps we have made the king make connections that simply are not there. Frantzen suggests that we cannot read a story that is not told, nor interpret a text that simply is not there: "the text on the sword-hilt is an episode no one has witnessed; likewise Hrothgar's own reading of the hilt offers no exegesis" (1990). Or perhaps, on the basis of the comprehensive symbolicity and temporal synthesis of his interpretation, the king has at least succeeded in defining a trajectory for the sword signs and we may identify, or tentatively assign a Final interpretant to, a definitive meaning, for the sword sign. This might be something like change, or death, or transience, or mortality—the kind of interpretant that rarely acknowledges "sufficient consideration" and does not lend itself to finite, tidy resolution.

The speech is certainly a multifaceted point of sign synthesis— regardless of who is doing the synthesizing and why—but its symbolic, contemplative stasis is essentially temporary. Whether we contemplate textual exegesis or textual *aporia*, the convergence of the coils of interlace generates the embryo of the continuing

Figure 4

Hrothgar's sermon: 1700–1784

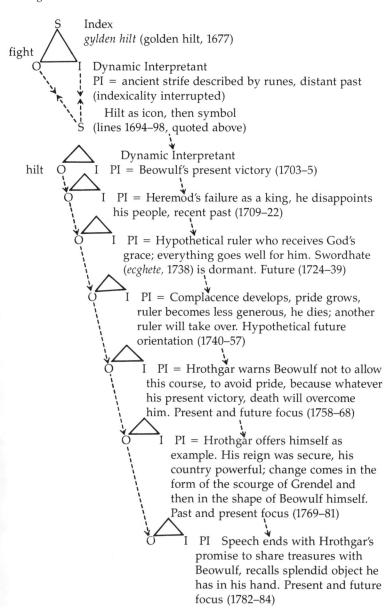

S   Index
gylden hilt (golden hilt, 1677)

fight

O   I   Dynamic Interpretant
PI = ancient strife described by runes, distant past
(indexicality interrupted)

Hilt as icon, then symbol
S (lines 1694–98, quoted above)

Dynamic Interpretant
hilt   O   I PI = Beowulf's present victory (1703–5)

O   I   PI = Heremod's failure as a king, he disappoints
his people, recent past (1709–22)

O   I   PI = Hypothetical ruler who receives God's
grace; everything goes well for him. Swordhate
(*ecghete*, 1738) is dormant. Future (1724–39)

O   I   PI = Complacence develops, pride grows,
ruler becomes less generous, he dies; another
ruler will take over. Hypothetical future
orientation (1740–57)

O   I   PI = Hrothgar warns Beowulf not to allow
this course, to avoid pride, because whatever
his present victory, death will overcome
him. Present and future focus (1758–68)

O   I   PI = Hrothgar offers himself as
example. His reign was secure, his
country powerful; change comes in the
form of the scourge of Grendel and
then in the shape of Beowulf himself.
Past and present focus (1769–81)

O   I PI Speech ends with Hrothgar's
promise to share treasures with
Beowulf, recalls splendid object he
has in his hand. Present and future
focus (1782–84)

pattern as it also leads back to whence it came. We stand at Niles's narrative "crossroads." We can finish the poet's task and tell an untold story for ourselves (always an option). We can either move on to hear Beowulf's version of events as he reports them to his lord Hygelac, a speech wherein the sword sign regains its bloody indexicality as the hero forecasts the failure of Hrothgar's attempts at peace-weaving occasioned by the sight of an old sword (2032–69). Or we can move back to Wealhtheow's speeches and the irresolvable ambiguity they engender.

The analysis of the following chapter shows how the queen's words spin a linguistic paradox of multipotential, essentially inconclusive interpretants, disrupting the possibilities for tele-ological direction and resolution. In fact, Hrothgar's speech offers several possibilities: a path out of, or back into, Secondness, the option of continuing to engage in the reciprocal semeiosis en-acted between reader and text, or of finishing the tale, stopping the journey. The path is neither straight nor circular, but a self-generating spiral always on the move. The Secondness in the poem is far from "dead"; "the fork in the road," writes Peirce, "is a third, it supposes three ways" (1: 337).

The nature of object-sign interaction, indeed sign interaction in general, in *Beowulf* demonstrates one of the ways in which this poem rests on the horns of a critical dilemma, or perhaps sits squarely on the fence between Secondness and Thirdness, bet-ween the dynamic viscerality of the index and the collected synthesis of the symbol, between the thing and the word, bet-ween experience and language.[24] The text neither fully succumbs to the self-presence, appropriation, or resolution—albeit tempor-ary—of the hermeneutic endeavor, nor to the deconstructionist freeplay of substitutions in the closure of a text as "finite ensem-ble." The object signs are always expanding, cross-referring, resonating, accruing, and continually translating meaning, break-ing the boundaries of the text as the spirals of interlace spill over the page. The dynamic semeiosis in the poem, paralleling the metonymic mode of its language, resists resolution and finitude, resists withdrawal into expression and a subsequent recourse to, and privileging of, the subject. If we posit continual semeiosis, a text without apparent end, to what extent must we abandon Peircean teleology, or the attempt to answer "the great questions of the poem"?

The poem offers its own solution, or rather, a mode of persis-tently shaping its own questions. Suppose we were to accept

Hrothgar's interpretation of the sword sign, or decide upon it as our own, there remains a curious isomorphism of mode and meaning in *Beowulf,* which I think may be one reason for the fascination it so persistently retains for readers. We can choose to assign a definitive meaning, a Final interpretant to the sword sign, and are then faced with elusive notions of death and transience. Broadly speaking, the signs of the whole poem add up to a similarly elusive total: we are back on Klaeber's "rambling, dilatory" path. The repetitions, convolutions, and wanderings of theme and structure might suggest that the entire poem is "about" process—the nature of change, social, moral, and mortal—perhaps a form of continual questioning and examination of values, heroic and Christian.

In one sense, then, the signs of this text are self-referential, in that their form, the sign interaction, is best characterized by the process of, even *as* a process of, questioning, revaluing—in effect, translation. The kinetic signs of this text display the same "inherent power of expansion" and restless energy reflected so clearly elsewhere in the period in the art form of interlace, where continuity inheres in the pattern.

If the signs of the poem are "about" process, however, Peirce would insist that we as interpreters of signs are a part of that process, that as subjects we too are in process. Peirce's assertion that the self is a product of signs is itself a sign within the continuum of semeiosis (5.313), anticipates more contemporary views on the problematic of self. In a letter to Lady Welby quoted earlier in this chapter, he comments: "I define a Sign as anything which is so determined by something else, called its object, and so determines an effect upon a person, which effect I call its Interpretant, that the latter is mediately determined by the former. My insertion of 'upon a person' is a sop to Cerberus, because I despair of making my own broader conception understood" (Hardwick, 80–81).

T. L. Short argues for the comprehensive breadth of Peirce's concept of semeiosis, and demonstrates that intentionality and significance are not dependent on human, conscious thought: "Peirce wished to analyze the human mind as a special case of semeiosis, rather than semeiosis as a special application of mind" (203). The notion that we are "in meaning," and not vice versa, which evolved in the preceding chapter's discussion of language, surfaces again. The important distinguishing characteristics of human semeiosis may be a "higher degree of self-correctiveness" and "the goal-directed creation and manipulation of signs as well as their goal-directed interpretation" (220), but the potential for teleological rigidity, as we have seen, is attentuated by Peirce's pragmatism; definitive meaning is a function of the habit of interpretation: "the most perfect account of a concept that words can convey will consist in a description of the habit which that concept is calculated to produce" (5.491). The "limits" of subjectivity are duly acknowledged, engaged, incorporated, one might say programmed into the semeiotic dynamic, as human semeiosis is also defined particularly in terms of change. In Shapiro's words, "Change as an aspect of continuity in human culture thus arises as a concomitant of the teleology of function in all semeiosis" (1983: 212).

Peirce's theory of signs comes close to the goal of all semiotics, which, according to Kristeva, should be to establish a kind of science of process, a descriptive methodology that engages but does not privilege the subject. Semiotics must continually postulate the heterogeneity of all types of systems without making pronouncements about them. As long as the speaking subject is itself understood as the subject of a heterogeneous process, Kristeva asserts that "semiotics can lead to a *historical typology of signifying practices* by the mere fact of recognizing the specific status within them of the speaking subject" (1986: 32), a typology that might fulfill the promise of dialectics that Peirce envisioned (Kristeva, 31). If we also see Kristeva's "speaking subject" or producer of signs as "spoken" or as a receiver, we are once more contemplating the problematic of self and the nature of desire: "As we use or receive signs, we produce interpretants. Their significate effects must pass through each of us, each body and each consciousness, before they produce an effect or an action upon the world. *The individual's habit as a semiotic production is both the result and the condition of the social production of meaning*" (de Lauretis, 1984: 173).

Peirce's theory of signs does not venture into psychological or psychoanalytic domains. Although the classes of interpretants cover an individual's emotions, physical energies, and logical capacities, de Lauretis reminds us that Peirce never "so much as suggests what kind of body it is, or how the body is itself produced as a sign *for* the subject" (1984: 183). The forces shaping our habits of interpretation or determining the angle of our

collateral observation are not directly addressed in Peirce's se-
meiotic. What it *can* offer directly is, above all, a nonreductive,
creative approach to analyzing and more clearly perceiving expe-
rience—linguistic, artistic, and otherwise. His concept of sign
offers a means of heterogenizing systems, a way of avoiding—or
re-creating—categories, like those of words and things, for exam-
ple, or in the case of *Beowulf*, of swords and signs.

Peirce's semeiotic reveals how the signs of the poem work, how
they can work upon us, how we translate and are translated by
them, how we are "spoken" by permission. It offers a vocabulary
and a means of discovery, as it crosses and conflates our catego-
ries of experience, and as it addresses those qualities of the poem
that have been previously perceived in art. Peirce's semeiotic can
conjure the persistent regenerative energy of movement and the
restlessness of dialectic—preoccupations of both the Anglo-Saxon
artist tracing the spirals of interlace, and of the following chapter,
which examines the potential of the poem's restless dialectics
from the points of view of gender and paradox.

Although Peirce's system stops short of addressing the nature
of the production of the self-sign, this chapter's examination of
the semiotic construction of meaning paves the way for the issues
to be addressed in the next chapter. Peirce's concepts of interpre-
tant and of semeiosis as ongoing, expansive process are central to
the problematic of desire and gender in that they "usher in a
theory of meaning as a continual cultural production that is not
only susceptible of ideological transformation, but materially
based in historical change" (de Lauretis, 1984: 172). The socio-
cultural moorings of semiotic meaning add the strands of cultur-
ally engendered desire operating within text and reader to the
web of interpretation reciprocally enacted/created by text and
reader, and so engender both the web of *différance* and the activity
of weaving.

3   Gender and Interpretation in *Beowulf*

> An impossible dialectic of two terms, a permanent alteration:
> never one without the other. It is not certain that someone is
> capable of it. . . . Perhaps, a woman. . . .
>
> Julia Kristeva, About Chinese Women

Voices for Paradox

Throughout the previous discussions of metonymic and semiotic
constructions of meaning, my aim has been to follow and de-
scribe levels of textual movement; both approaches image the web
of *différance* in that they insist on the elements of open-endedness
and ongoing process, and both offer a critical apparatus that can
trace or parallel aspects of the complex dynamic of *Beowulf.* The
play of difference as it is described by the operation of metonymy
or by the continual translation of signs remains relatively abstract
in that it may exist, if we permit it to do so, as theoretically
discrete, distanced from social, psychical, or sexual motivations,
untainted by the problematic of desire. However, both metonymic
and semiotic constructs beg the questions that this chapter will
begin to address. The questions, as we have already seen, are
hard to articulate separately. At the conclusion of chapter 1, the
concept of metonymy did not resolve into a clear critical meth-
odology, but raised the questions of whether the Old English
poetic text is metonymic, whether I or any reader desires that it be
metonymic, or whether, according to Lacan, desire is a series of
metonymies anyway. A metonymic construction of desire, more-
over, evokes a sexual dimension, within or without the text. Jane
Gallop and others call attention to the parallels between meta-
phor/metonymy and masculine unitary/feminine fragmentary
expressions of desire.[1] The semiotic argument of chapter 2 de-
scribes reader and text in an ongoing collaborative dynamic; signs

are products of users, users are products of signs, but we may also ask what or who is producing the subject as user or the subject as speaker or producer of signs.

Although the questions of what produces desire and what desire produces remain inextricably interwoven, it is possible to trace several of these interconnected strands for temporarily separate examination. To ask a question, de Lauretis suggests, is itself a question of desire, but "a story too is always a question of desire" and we can ask "whose desire is it that speaks, and whom does that desire address?" (1984: 112).

In this chapter I shall focus primarily on the operation of desire within the narrative, on the ways in which desire is directed, redirected, and conflicted in *Beowulf.* My aim, which is still to address the complexity and dynamism of the poem in a manner consonant with the terms of its difference, is well served by the introduction of the problematic of desire, which not only engages and incorporates the patterns of intersection discovered by metonymic and semiotic approaches, but adds another yet more complex strand to the web of interpretation. Marginal desire in *Beowulf,* whether this is monstrous, feminine, or even heroic, continually intrudes upon and deflects the progress of dominant desire, and this process offers an overarching context for the restless dynamic of the poem. The operation of desire offers another means of envisioning how one and two never comfortably resolve into a ranked pair, or become, finally, three—another response to my students' comment that it's so hard to keep the whole poem in your mind at the same time.

How, then, may we characterize dominant desire in the poem in order to examine its restless dialectic with marginal desire? Who wants what in *Beowulf* and who gets it? At first, and even second glance, *Beowulf* seems to be a poem about death: how to die, how to seek out death, how to meet it head on, how to get it before it gets you, how to glory in defiant incomprehension of it, how to make it so commonplace that it becomes an old familiar, how to choose it, privilege it, embrace it. Everywhere in the poem this deathly embrace spawns a variety of forms of closure, a continual need for resolution, the notion that choice is heroic, inescapable, and reducible to simple binary oppositions—one or the other. And the other always loses.

Not unexpectedly, Beowulf is also an overwhelmingly masculine poem; it could be seen as a chronicle of male desire, a tale of men dying. In the masculine economy[2] of the poem, desire expresses itself as desire for the other, as a continual process of subjugation and appropriation of the other. The code of vengeance and the heroic choice demand above all a *resolution* of opposing elements, a decision must always be made. Consider the story Beowulf tells about his grandfather Hrethel: Haethcyn, his second son, accidentally kills Herebeald, his first son; vengeance is necessary—one death must pay for another—but impossible in this case; the old man cannot, will not, survive in the in-between of indecision; he gives up all joy in life (*gumdream ofgeaf,* 2469), withers away and dies himself. All "choice" leads to death.

In *Beyond the Pleasure Principle,* Freud equates the logical end, the ultimate object of all desire, with actual death. A psychoanalytic understanding of desire as deferred death, of the symbolic nature of desire in action, is often not necessary in *Beowulf*; death is continually present, always in the poem's foreground: the hero says "I will do this or I will die." Resolution, choice, satisfaction of desire frequently mean literal death. On a less extreme level, the closure that desire-as-appropriation involves is just that: a shutting down of the dialectic of oppositions, of differences, of others; a foretaste of the grand closure of death.

Silverman characterizes the Freudian concept of desire as/for death as a "notion of pleasure as a zero-degree of tension" (57), and though we must concede that there is a lot of death and need for resolution in *Beowulf,* we must also recognize that there is a great deal of tension. One can find places in the narrative where the poet actually *prefers* tension to resolution, the process of making the decision to the decision accomplished.[3] As the poem escapes closure and resolution in a variety of ways already examined, it also escapes the "dead end" of masculine desire. The metonymic mode of language in the poem is partially responsible for the poem's vibrant, immediate, and peculiarly life-related qualities; although the world of *Beowulf* is well characterized by Peirce's category of Secondness, this quality of Secondness is not "dead"; it is not simply dyadic, nor does it preclude the possibility of Thirdness, the movement into symbolicity and synthesis. I have also demonstrated how the poem's structure, or the ways in which the signs of the text cohere, embodies the restless, kinetic mode of interlace, an artistic mode alien to closure, where resolution is resisted by inherent dynamism and expansion. There are other elements in the poem that speak for desire as life, elements of marginal desire that disrupt the dominant discourse, that escape appropriation and operate against resolution in a simple, binary sense. Who, what are these others, what is "other" in *Beowulf*?

A genuine "Other," in Hélène Cixous and Catherine Clément's terms, cannot be theorized, "it doesn't settle down" (71). Nevertheless, they continue, historically "what is called 'other' is an alterity that does settle down, that falls into the dialectical circle. It is the other in a hierarchically organized relationship in which the same is what rules, defines, and assigns 'its' other" (71). In the byzantine tribal feuds, the repeated reconfiguration of enmity and alliance in *Beowulf,* we see the continual production of the other as reproduction of the same, of the master/slave dialectic. Such alterity is assimilated into the binary status quo, feeds on resolution, indeed demonstrates the "dreadful simplicity that orders the movement Hegel erected as a system" (Cixous and Clément, 71). The monsters, of course, as more seriously alien, hint at an unrealizable, genuine alterity; they temporarily disrupt, even confuse the apparently inexorable process of assimilation and reappropriation. The metonymic mode of language and the dynamic semiosis of interlace, discussed in chapters 1 and 2, are both factors that contribute to the life-related qualities of the poem. But the dynamism of this poem is also a function of that which transcends, or rather resists, binary opposition and resolution, of an otherness that resides in paradox.

I have suggested that the elements of otherness, or of marginal desire, can be monstrous, feminine, and even heroic; the ambiguous "perhaps" in my introductory quotation from Kristeva suggests that the capacity to participate in an "impossible dialectic" is not limited to women. But in this study I want to pay most attention to the feminine for several reasons. Because of their connection to weaving—their function and activity as "peaceweavers"—women add a particularly interesting dimension to my overarching metaphor of weaving, and they, unlike the monsters, allow us to remain within the margins of human discourse. Also, they use language: the otherness that is generated in paradox is most clearly located in the voices of those ongoing manifestations of paradox, the women of *Beowulf,* and in the related concept of the advent of, or cultural initiation into, language embodied in the poem.

I should note here that by "voices" I also mean a more general idea of presence and function, including speech, gesture, and silence; there are several profoundly silent women in this poem. Also, the concept of language, taken up in my examination of Queen Wealhtheow, will enter the discussion in its simplest sense, as the counterpart or opposite to the mute regime of violence and action, as speech versus nonspeech.

There is no place for women in the masculine economy of *Beowulf*; they have no space to occupy, to claim, to speak from. The terms of psychoanalysis have a peculiar clarity and literality of application in this context. Lacan's construct, the Name-of-the-Father, engenders the Symbolic order, the Law, which is "an arbitrary order of abstraction whose power derives from the threat of castration as signified by the phallus" (in Cixous and Clément, 168).[4] The arbitrary nature of this order, the advent of which Freud saw as a "victory of spirituality over the senses," and "a declaration in favour of the thought-process,"[5] stems from paternal doubt: "The legal assignation of a Father's Name to a child is meant to call a halt to uncertainty about the identify of the father. If the mother's femininity . . . were affirmed, the Name-of-the-Father would always be in doubt, always be subject to the question of the mother's morality. Thus the Name-of-the-Father must be arbitrarily and absolutely imposed, thereby instituting the reign of patriarchal law" (Gallop, 1982: 39).

Lacan's construct "sustains the concept of desire with the structure of the law," (Lacan, 1981: 34) and also serves to connect the father and his name as a means of associating patriarchy with language: "the patronym, patriarchal law, patrilineal identity, language as our inscription into patriarchy. The Name-of-the-Father is the fact of the attribution of paternity by law, by language" (Gallop, 47). Paternal identification becomes the necessary condition for the subject's identification and entry into the world, a condition that caused Lacan to repeatedly state that "woman does not exist."[6]

The Name-of-the-Father functions on several literal and symbolic levels in *Beowulf*, underscoring the elements of exclusivity and homosexuality—here I refer to love of the same as a means of developing solidarity against the other, a primary bond, which may be social, emotional, or sexual, which is exclusively masculine. (I am putting aside for the moment the issue of language as an inscription into patriarchy.) Most obviously there is a tremendous preoccupation with genealogy in *Beowulf*; the father always identifies the son and daughter; the son is then identified by name. Often the women in the poem are not identified other than as daughters, wives, or mothers. Of the eleven women in the poem we know the names of five: Wealhtheow, Freawaru (both of which Eliason thinks are only nicknames, 1975: 10), Hygd, Hildeburh, and Modthryth/Thryth. These are, notably, all queens, with some titular power of rule. Beowulf's mother, a woman lauded as fortunate in her childbearing, remains nameless, in sharp contrast to his father Ecgtheow, who is mentioned sixteen times. Healfdene's daughter (King Hrothgar's sister) is mentioned in a problematic, much-amended part of the manuscript; Eliason advises against contriving an emendation for her name based on two considerations: the poet's "usual avoidance of women's names and his apparent unconcern about daughters" (Eliason, 9). Hygelac's only daughter is given to Eofor, slayer of Ongentheow, as reward for his battle prowess, along with land and rings (2993–97). Ongentheow's wife is shuttled back and forth in the battle between the Geats and the Swedes; a nameless Geatish woman mourns at the end of the poem. And, finally, there is Grendel's unnamed mother; barely identifiable as human, she also makes a doubtful female:

> Đæra oðer wæs,   Þæs þe hie gewislicost
> gewitan meahton,   idese onlicnes   (1349–51)

(one of them was, to the extent that they were able to make out with any certainty, in the likeness of a woman)

Her son, too, is a doubtful male, not just because of his monstrous appearance but also because the human community does not know who his father is (*no hie fæder cunnon*, 1355). (The poet, of course, identifies them both as the misshapen progeny of Cain in lines 1265–66.) The certainty of maternity, overwhelming in the case of this outraged dam, will not suffice to inscribe Grendel into the patriarchal symbolic order prevailing in the Danish court.

These fatherless monsters and nameless women have no place, no condition for entry into the symbolic order at the most literal level. The process of exclusion, moreover, operates with increasing complexity in the case of those named queens who speak and act, who have, ostensibly, a role to play in the poem. Acquiring a "place" through marriage does not guarantee identification; in fact, it can be a major force for exclusion. Robinson has noted the absence of "love" or "romantic passion between the sexes" in *Beowulf,* and throughout most Old English poetry (1984: 118–19). The secondary nature of the emotional marital bond provides a possible explanation for the hero's apparent celibacy. While scholars have pondered over Beowulf's marital status, Robinson suggests that the poet might simply have considered that "Beowulf's marital status was of insufficient interest to warrant mention in the poem" (119).

While we have no way of guessing at Beowulf's sexuality, or at the poet's or the hero's personal views on marriage, we cannot ignore the strength of expressed masculine desire in the poem. Intensity and passion are located in the bonds of loyalty and friendship forged between men, and marriage is valued as an extension of this larger emotional context. In *Beowulf* the marriage alliance is essentially an alliance of men; Deleuze and Guattari identify "the perverse tie of a primary homosexuality," a love of, even an obsession with, the "same" as a means of avoidance of the other, in tribal negotiation for marriage partners: "Through women, men establish their own connections; through the man-woman disjunction, which is always the outcome of filiation, alliance places in connection men from different filiations" (165). That such filiation often fails in *Beowulf* as a result of incessant feuding does not change the fact that the woman given in marriage is perceived as the visible token of male alliance.

The role of "peace-weaver" is one of the most familiar and best defined roles for women in *Beowulf* and throughout Old English poetry; it is also one of the most problematic, and I shall take it up at greater length in my discussion of Hildeburh. Here I want to emphasize that the most outstanding characteristic of the peace-weaver, especially as we see her in *Beowulf,* is her inevitable failure to *be* a peace-weaver; the task is never accomplished, the role is never fully assumed, the woman is never identified. The system of masculine alliance allows women to signify in a system of apparent exchange, but does not allow them signification in their own right—that is, outside the system of signification; they must be continually translated by and into the binary language of the prevailing masculine symbolic order. It is, as we shall see, an essentially untenable position, predicated on absence; but it also breeds paradox, a major means of deflecting/redirecting desire away from death.

The peace-weaving role also opens up a more complex perspective on weaving as *différance.* The play of absence and presence is

imaged in these supposedly "active" weavers of lines of connec-
tion between tribes and between stories within the text, whose
actual presence is shadowy, barely discernible. They enact *and*
embody the process of weaving, they weave and are woven by the
ties of kinship. The identification of women with the kinship
system is made clear by a linguistic equation; Earl points out that
the "terms most used to denote these kindreds in Old English are
mæg and *mægth*, which, not coincidentally, are homonymous if not
identical with the words for 'woman'" (1983: 143). Earl also
suggests that women as embodiments of kinship are simul-
taneously identified with its opposite, as "the warrior class . . .
identified the prime source of internal violence as the kinship
system and so justified its attack on the kindred" (146). Earl's
Freudian argument, which develops the opposition of women/
kinship/family to the masculine business of civilization, demon-
strates the cultural process by which women become "other,"[7]
underscoring the weaver's paradoxical complicity in the destruc-
tion of the web.

Enacting the ties of kinship, weaving the web of peace in
Beowulf, is a task of infinite regression, a never-ending process
that accurately reflects Derrida's concept of *différance* in that it
involves the dual attributes of deferral and absence of resolution,
and the attendant presence of a multitude of possibilities, a state
of infinite potential. Taking the side of possibility and preferring,
as I have outlined in the Introduction, to see this open-ended
"glass" as half-full, I shall argue that these weavers serve poten-
tial; they extend and revalue the multidirectionality of the web.

The women in *Beowulf,* whether illegitimate monsters or ped-
igreed peace-weaving queens, are all marginal, excluded figures;
they resemble, to differing extents, the figure of the "hysteric" as
this is employed by Cixous and Clément in their considerably
expanded and revalued definition of Freud's term. The hysteric is
one of society's anomalies, one of the "abnormal ones," a category
encompassing "madmen, deviants, neurotics, women, drifters,
jugglers, tumblers" (9), those who fall between the cracks of the
symbolic system. To this list we could easily add monsters and
heroes, especially if we recall the double sense of *wrecca* in *Beowulf*
as "exile" and "hero." Their alienated status allows and invites
society to make special demands on these anomalous individuals:
in Lévi-Strauss's terms, "the group asks and even compels these
people to represent certain forms of compromise, unrealizable on

the collective level, to simulate imaginary transitions, to embody incompatible syntheses" (in Cixous and Clément, 7). Women, in particular, are "all decked-out" in such contradictions: "more than any others, women bizarrely embody this group of anomalies showing the cracks in an overall system" (7). The hysteric's essential quality is that of ambiguity: Is she a heroine or victim, does she dismantle or reinforce the structures that contain her?

Throughout *The Newly Born Woman* (*La Jeune Née*), Cixous and Clément conduct a dialogue of definition that is not, cannot be, resolved. Cixous asserts that "the hysteric, with her way of questioning others . . . is, to my eyes, the typical woman in all her force . . . a force capable of demolishing those structures" (154). Clément agrees that the voice of the hysteric "introduces dissension, but it doesn't explode anything at all" (156); it can never bring about change in the symbolic order. But the presence of the hysteric demands a continual confrontation with unresolvable ambiguity: "there is no place for the hysteric; she cannot be placed or take place. Hysteria is necessarily an element that disturbs arrangements" (156).

In differing degrees of intensity, the women of *Beowulf* provide such a disturbance. While they do not figure in, let alone overturn, the symbolic order in the poem, they embody Kristeva's "impossible dialectic," an insistent paradox that is part of the poem's affinity with life, and its eventual rejection of desire as death.

Critical Voices

Characterizing the women of *Beowulf* as hysterics not only allies them with ambiguity, but is also a means of avoiding a reductive critical approach. Before examining the "hysterical" potential of some of the poem's female characters, and their capacity to disrupt its binary dynamic, it would be customary and informative to look at some other critical views of women in *Beowulf* and in Old English poetry as a whole. But in this case it is also important to my argument to show that there has been a perhaps equally overwhelming binarism coming from without the poem. The push for definition and resolution, often resulting in reductive either/or classification, is reflected with most alarming clarity and rigidity in critical assessments of women, not only in *Beowulf* but in Old English poetry in general.

Following an examination of his initial generalization that "the women of Anglo-Saxon secular poetry endure something more than their rightful share of discomfort" (1975: 224), Alain Renoir postulates the "existence of a tradition of suffering women" (235). This gives rise to a degree of expectation on the part of the audience and compliance on the part of the poet. In other words, female suffering and passivity are forms of poetic givens, and the more or less casual nature of their acceptance is well described by Renoir's analogy: "The principle invoked here is the same which applies to ethnic jokes in modern America: though the members of a given audience may never have been directly exposed to this particular brand of entertainment before, enough of them will have heard about it to lead the others tacitly into expecting the humor to be at the expense of some ethnic group and responding accordingly" (236).

Renoir posits one extreme, that of the passive, suffering victim, as the female norm in secular poetry.[8] This widespread critical view has been developed in a variety of ways. Anne Klinck looks at several secular and Christian poems and finds "a definite pattern traceable through Old English poetry," in which "the female character is confined and restricted" (605), literally, emotionally, and by convention. Klinck manages to transform this rather gruesome state of affairs into a happy, artistic accident; passivity is productive psychological material as one form of exploitation spawns another: "Women characters can be exploited in subtler and more searching ways than male characters in the conventional heroic situations. Simply because women are debarred from action, their position becomes psychologically more interesting. . . . Because the poets are treating an area not provided for in the poetic conventions, they are forced back upon observation and intuition instead of literary precedent" (606).

Klinck makes a virtue out of what is perceived as a necessity, and discovers poetic virtue and vitality in the norm of female passivity. Elaine Tuttle Hansen takes yet another compensatory approach and emphasizes the moral function of this inevitable and pitiable, but nonetheless educational, passivity. She asserts that one of the aspects of the Germanic woman most emphasized in poetic tradition is her "greater share in human suffering and anguish" (111), but that this extreme has a moral implication. In *Beowulf* there is a "dramatic contrast between the feminine ideal, a civilizing, ordering force, and the underlying weakness of woman's moral and social powers in the face of the irrepressible evils in man and his society" (113). If female suffering functions as a

moral directive on the one hand, it is also seen as totally ineffec-
tive on the other: one form of passivity spawns another.

No one can deny that women suffer a great deal in Old English
poetry. What I am objecting to in these arguments is the basic
conceptual assumption of woman as passive, suffering victim,
which is then placed in binary opposition to, and measured
against, male aggressivity. Men are violent, women are weak; the
other is always destroyed, literal death or the closure of desire-as-
appropriation will always prevail. This denies the power of the
hysteric and the vitality of the poetry, especially of *Beowulf.* Many,
perhaps all, the women in *Beowulf* do not qualify as "civilizing,
ordering" forces in the sense that they cannot be defined or even
perceived in contrast to the masculine economy that negates
them; they resist simple definition by contrast, by means of
opposition. This point is made curiously clear in the case of Old
English Christian poems, where the women "disappears" com-
pletely, leaving no trace even in paradox.

The female saints and martyrs of the Christian poems are often
seen as active rather than passive, their suffering transformed
into an aggressive triumph: "for the first time we meet females
who do not suffer as symbols of man's impotence in the face of
wyrd, but who are triumphant saints and heroes fighting for the
true faith and thus empowered to overcome the limitations of both
their sex and their unaided mortality" (Hansen, 117). The almost
ghoulish aspect of the series of distortions/contortions involved
here is hinted at by Renoir; his generalization about secular
female misery does not apply to this set of women: "There, the
opposite principle applies more often than not, so that we may
find a Juliana's disposition 'greatly cheered' (*micclum geblissad*) at
the prospect of her own demise" (1975: 224). Desire for death,
desire as death, annihilates these saintly women.

In *Woman as Hero in Old English Literature,* Jane Chance demon-
strates the ways in which both the heroic status and Christian
approbation of women are absolutely attendant upon chastity:
"The protagonists of the religious epics—Juliana, Judith, Elene—
exemplify degrees of chastity from pure virginity (Juliana) to
chaste widowhood (Judith) and chaste conjugality (Elene). Each
illustrates heroic behavior through sanctity" (xv); one becomes a
condition for the other. This principle extends well beyond poetry
to the public domain. Women with public positions and political
power, of whom there were a considerable number in the Anglo-

Saxon period,[9] were "permitted an active political role in king-
doms as chaste rulers or strong abbesses, and some became saints
who were even allowed to adopt heroic behavior (even masculine
clothing) once their chastity and sanctity had been attested"
(Chance, xv). Women who attempted to use power in any way
without this "'armor' . . . were usually castigated as lascivious,
immoral, and even diabolic" (Chance, 53).

The premise at work here is apparent; the escape from passivity
may only be accomplished by a denial of sexuality, an obliteration
of femininity. Chance's study makes this point clear, but the
critical view of Christian women as aggressive, triumphant, or
somehow vindicated overlooks the patristic invention of necessity
for their absence (that is, Eve as responsible for evil) and glosses
over their complicity in their own disappearance. It reaffirms
either/or binarism, while simply reconfiguring its elements: wo-
men may be not-weak as long as they are not-women.

Whether or not the patristic view of the evil of women leads
eventually to their legal and social decline later in the Anglo-
Saxon period, as some recent historians have suggested,[10] it does
guarantee their very literal effacement in much of Christian
poetry. But the specter of denied or repressed sexuality does not
haunt secular poetry with such finality and drastic oversim-
plification. A "trace," in Derrida's terms, of the woman (or woman
as trace) may still be discovered, provided that one is prepared to
find it through absence, and in the play of paradox: "the trace is
not a presence but is rather a simulacrum of a presence that
dislocates, displaces, and refers beyond itself. The trace has,
properly speaking, no place, for effacement belongs to the very
structure of the trace" (Derrida, 1973: 156). We can identify the
trace of the women of *Beowulf* in this continual process of efface-
ment ("one tracks down tracks" —Derrida, 158), the very process
denied those saints and martyrs, whose hysteric potential is
absorbed and ratified, and who are so far assimilated into the
patriarchal, Christian, symbolic order that they leave no trace
whatsoever.

One other critical voice merits attention: that which seeks to
reexamine the assumption of female passivity in secular poetry.
There have been several recent attempts to create a different
context for the discussion of women and women's roles.[11] One of
the most interesting is Helen Damico's *Beowulf's Wealhtheow and
the Valkyrie Tradition*. Rejecting traditional critical views of Wealh-

theow as a tragic or ironic victim, idealized queen or ornamental figure, Damico argues for the literality of her position as a powerful political force in the poem. She identifies *Beowulf*'s most important female as a valkyrie figure, and marshals historical and textual evidence to support her claim. This argument is initially attractive because it acknowledges and validates the sense one has of the power and enigmatic presence of this woman, the only one who actually speaks in the poem. Damico allows her the menacing, ambiguous authority of the valkyrie, the chooser of the slain and cupbearer to the Gods; she interprets Beowulf and Wealhtheow's meeting in the Danish court as "the archetypal first encounter between a valkyrie and a hero" (67). In true valkyrie fashion, Wealhtheow charges the hero with his heroic destiny when she offers him the cup, and fulfills her own desire at the same time. She incites the hero to his own possible death in order to help him forge his heroic "immortal" identity.

Damico's interesting argument, to which I shall return in my own discussion of Wealhtheow, nonetheless raises some difficult questions. Aside from the potential problem of her working backward, in that the Scandinavian sources postdate *Beowulf* by at least two hundred years,[12] there is a reactionary backlash inherent in some aspects of this vision of the queen. Is Wealhtheow's power truly active and self-generated? The valkyrie offers death, embodies contact with death; her semireligious, priestess function gives her tremendous power as the repository of masculine fears and ambivalence. She represents a kind of "making holy" or mythologizing of the code of violence, self-destruction, and desire-as-appropriation, and also provides an external focus for ambivalence. As death fulfills her own desire as well as that of the hero, she may blamed or praised, despised or adored, feared or welcomed. The valkyrie essentially *participates* in the death-centered, male definition of power, and is finally a vehicle for its consummation—another variety of victim, another version of woman as death-and-salvation for men, another assimilated hysteric.

Renoir's vision of pathetic, inevitable female passivity may appear to contrast with Damico's vision of menacing, semireligious power, but both views are subsumed by the premise of passivity on a much broader scale: that is, female participation in male, death-centered desire. Although the ambiguity of the valkyrie figure makes it difficult to net her in simple opposition, to claim conclusively or confidently that she is either/or, my point is finally whether or not she must be netted, or allowed to escape the limitations of binary definition. Whether or not ambiguity may be tolerated, even affirmed, as a condition for "tracing" Wealhtheow and her counterparts in *Beowulf* will be central to the following discussions.

I intend to focus on just three of the women in the poem, chosen for the variety and degree of disturbance they provide in their roles as hysterics. The profoundly silent Hildeburh is an interesting counterpart to the language-wielding Wealhtheow; both offer individual versions of hysteria as well as illuminating each other's function in the poem. Much of what can be said about these two women may also apply by implication to the poem's other human females, who are mentioned only in passing by the poet. I have chosen not to discuss Grendel's mother separately precisely because she is not quite human, or, rather, she has her own particular brand of otherness; her inhuman affiliation and propensities make it hard to distinguish between what is monstrous and what is female—a complication I considered less than useful to my argument. My third choice is Modthryth, the brevity of whose appearance in the poem is in surprising contrast to the extent and impact of her hysterical contribution.

The Helenization of Hildeburh

Queen Hildeburh, whom Renoir calls "by far the most unfortunate human being in *Beowulf*" (1975: 230), is a victim par excellence, but her presence serves to indict the system that ostensibly champions her as its cause, and to expose its paradoxical demands. She has much in common with the legendary Helen as the designated female focal point of a masculine system of exchange, or more accurately, of appropriation: "Men say that it is for her that the Greeks launched a thousand ships, destroyed, killed, waged a fabulous war for ten-times-ten years—among men! For the sake of her, yonder, the idol, carried off, hidden, lost. Because it is for-her and without-her that they live it up at the celebration of death that they call their life" (Cixous and Clément, 70).

Hildeburh's story is told to the Danish court by Hrothgar's scop, as part of the "entertainment in the hall" (*healgamen*, 1066) following Beowulf's first victory over the monster Grendel. She is married to Finn, a Frisian king, as a pledge of peace between Frisians and Danes. When her brother Hnaef comes to visit her (or possibly to look for trouble) at Finn's court, a fight breaks out and he is killed, along with her son by Finn. In the next round of fighting, led by Hengest, Hnaef's faithful retainer who cannot rest until he avenges the death of his lord, Finn is killed off, and the sorrowful queen hauled victoriously back across the sea to her people along with other prizes of treasure and war spoils. Queen loses all. This is her story in a nutshell, though the poet's narrative technique is a key factor in explaining its powerful, psychological effect.[13]

In the Finn episode Hildeburh has nothing to say; we hear the echo, or follow the trace, of her speech when we are told that she gave the order for her son to be burned on the same funeral pyre as her brother (1114–16), and that she lamented with songs (*geomrode giddum*, 1118) as the smoke wound upward. Both gestures may seem to associate her with passivity or death; one a kind of acquiescence to the equanimity of its embrace, the other directly (or indexically, according to the Peircean argument of chapter 2) to the nameless Geatish woman who laments with mournful song (*giomorgyd*, 3150) as the smoke rises from Beowulf's pyre at the end of the poem. She thus participates in a scarcely interrupted dirge of female sorrow and impotence. In addition to the loss of husband, brother, son, and home, Chance asserts that she also mourns her own failure, heaping self-blame upon impotence in a positive conundrum of death and defeat:

All she does, this sad woman, is to mourn her loss with dirges. . . . In fact, she can do nothing, caught in the very web she has woven as peace pledge . . . the peace pledge must accept a passive role precisely because the ties she knots bind *her*—she *is* the knot, the pledge of peace. Her fate interlaces with that of her husband and brothers through her role as a mother bearing a son: thus Hildeburh appropriately mourns the loss of her symbolic tie at the pyre, the failure of her self as peace pledge, the loss of her identity. (100)

Chance's assessment of Hildeburh's situation may be at odds with a point she stresses elsewhere—that of the basic untenability of the role of peace-weaver—as well as overlooking the fact that Hildeburh cannot lose an identity she never possessed in the first place.

Peace-weavers are assigned the role of creating peace, in fact, embodying peace, in a culture where war and death are privileged values. Female failure is built into this system, as Chance clearly demonstrates in an ostensibly different context. In her discussion of Eve in *Genesis B,* Chance rationalizes her failure to withstand temptation on grounds that resemble the recent socio-linguistic notion of "trained incapacity" in female language use.[14] Satan represents eating the apple to Eve as part of an attempt to make peace between God and Adam, to avert enmity between them, which would ensue if Adam disobeys Satan, who poses as God's retainer. When Eve finally agrees, she is accepting her role as peace-weaver. "Thus Eve fails here not because she is unintelligent or inferior to Adam but because she has not been trained to resist, to fight, to remain strong against an adversary, and because this 'best of women' in an Anglo-Saxon society would have been trained instead to concede, to ameliorate, to harmonize" (Chance, 74).

One of the less publicized but perhaps equally dire results of Eve's peace-weaving is that she persists in trying to assume the role, to do the impossible; later in the poem she weaves clothing for the naked pair, an act that prefigures the "heavenly weaving" (Chance, 79), or intercession, of the Virgin Mary. Eve, the Virgin Mary, and the Germanic woman are all located in a continuum of perpetual aspiration to fulfill the role of peace-weaver; the Virgin's relative success may spur on "the peace-weaver who has failed but who will continue in succeeding centuries to toil for peace between family members and between tribes, weaving through words and offspring what the First Peace-weaver attempted through her disobedient eating of the fruit and her later weaving of leaves into suitable covering for the pair" (Chance, 79). This sweeping vision of female failure through the ages to come bears an uncanny obverse resemblance to Milton's prophesy concerning female "perverseness" in *Paradise Lost*: "Which infinite calamity shall cause to human life, and household peace confound" (Book X, 907–8).

Perversity is certainly one of the key elements in Hildeburh's situation, and is not unrelated to paradox. The inevitable failure and essential untenability of her female role is even affirmed by the hero himself. When he returns to Hygelac's court, Beowulf tells his lord of Hrothgar's attempt to make peace with the Heathobards by marrying his daughter Freawaru to Ingeld, prince of the Heathobards (2020–69). Beowulf constructs a scenario, visualizes the details of Freawaru's failure: at a scene of feasting in the hall presided over by the young couple, an old Heathobard warrior will become incensed at the sight of a young Dane flaunting battle gear stripped from dead Heathobard warriors; the old man cannot rest until Freawaru's thane (*se fæmnan þegn*, 2059) is dead, and the feud is renewed. Such bitter hatred, comments Beowulf, is bound to diminish Ingeld's love for his bride: *ond him wiflufan / æfter cearwælmum colran weorðað* (and his love for his wife, through such seethings of sorrow, will become cooler, 2065–66). Moreover, Beowulf generalizes, feuds are seldom settled by peace-weaving, whatever the individual worth of the woman involved: *þeah seo bryd duge!* (*however right the bride!*, 2031; my italics, Klaeber's exclamation point).

Beowulf's story is interesting for several reasons. The sensitivity and accuracy of his understanding are remarkable in this scene as they are when he tells the story of his anguished grandfather, Hrethel. It is no small part of the poem's power and attraction that its hero is also a thinker, that he is polite (witness his tact with the Danish coastguard), and intelligent (witness his strategic assessment of Grendel's method of attack), and that he suffers from recognizable neuroses (witness his wondering what he had done to deserve the scourge of the dragon). The most accomplished binarist in the poem (I will do *x* or I will die), Beowulf is also aware of the often agonizing circumstances of coming to a decision. This duality in the hero suggests some of his own potential as a hysteric; even as he functions as an epitome of the binary heroic standard, he is also calling it into question and pointing out its limitations.

The hero himself is one of the most unsettling forces in the poem and has long been recognized for the kinds of ambiguity he generates—about the value of pagan and Christian ideals or the value of treasure, for example. His power to disturb as a hysteric accrues throughout the poem; when Beowulf, the accomplished, one might say professional, binarist, finally chooses death fully understanding the terms of the choice, he calls attention to the illusion of choice and the illusion of the power of the subject to make it. Beowulf's barrow remains a profoundly ambiguous reminder of a life and a death. The important difference, however, between the hero as hysteric and some of the women in the poem is that he *does* choose death—unlike Hildeburh or the nameless mourner who laments over the barrow.[15] He may question, disrupt, or challenge the symbolic order, but eventually he opts for resolution. In this regard, he has something in common with Modthryth, who becomes, as we shall see, an assimilated hysteric— she rocks the boat, challenges the dominant symbolic order for a while, but then settles down. The hero's understanding of process must always culminate in resolution, the capacity for which is a condition of heroism in this binary, death-centered context, but the added complexity and hysterical potential of Beowulf's heroic character, while it is an unsettling force in its own right, also comments on the nature of binarism in the poem and women's paradoxical relation to it.

The hero's description and prophesy of Freawaru's failure is almost casually included in his account of his Danish adventures; it is one of those regular and regrettable facts of Germanic daily life, one that not only reveals the totality of female exclusion but diagrams the terms of their nonsignification. The system of male alliance that negates Freawaru and Hildeburh is one of appropriation, not exchange: "Desire knows nothing of exchange, *it knows only theft and gift,* at times the one within the other under the effect of a primary homosexuality" (Deleuze and Guattari, 186).

The primary bond, in both social and emotional, and possibly sexual terms, is exclusively masculine, and therefore precludes any possibility of genuine exchange, which must take into account the other, the feminine, as an actual, realized entity. As these female peace-weavers are taken and given, stolen or discarded, their potential currency, their function, their power to signify is removed. I have argued that elsewhere in the poem there is a peculiar interchangeability of words, deeds, and things,[16] but this flow of signification stops short of, or with, the women in the poem. The sword may recall the boast that may assure the deed; objects have an almost palpable presence. But even the gold adorning the queen will not translate *her*; it may be an index, in Peircean terms, to renewed strife—that is, it may translate into war, into the currency of the masculine economy, but her meaning as peace-weaver is *untranslatable.* The "language" of women is not spoken here.

With this argument for the silence, the utter nonsignification of the women as peace-weaver, to some extent revealed and authorized by the hero himself, I return to the "unfortunate" Hildeburh. Her spectacular failure evokes far more than pity. Her silence and absence create an even more profound silence within the poem. Into the noisy merriment, the *sang and sweg* of Hrothgar's court, her story falls like a solitary pebble; the focus of the beginning, center, and conclusion of the poet's song is the queen. She is immediately introduced by name, her father's name men-

tioned several lines later as a secondary means of identification.
The story begins from her vantage point, and describes what she
saw, what she may have thought and felt:

> Ne huru Hildeburh   herian þorfte
> Eotena treowe;   unsynnum weard
> beloren leofum   æt þam lindplegan
> bearnum and brodrum;   hie on gebyrd hruron
> gare wunde;   þaet wæs geomuru ides!
> Nalles holinga   Hoces dohtor
> meotodsceaft bemearn,   syþdan morgen com,
> da heo under swegle   geseon meahte
> morþorbealo maga,   þær heo ær mæste heold
> worolde wynne.   (1071–80)

(Indeed Hildeburh had no need to praise the good faith of the Jutes.
Guiltlessly, she was deprived of her loved ones, son and brother, at
the play of shields; they fell fated, wounded by the spear. That was a
sad woman! Not without cause did Hoc's daughter lament the decree of
fate when morning came, and she was able to see beneath the sky the
slaughter of her kinsmen, where before she had held most of her
worldly joy.)

After the first round of fighting the poet returns to her, to
report her gesture of conciliation, a kind of peace-weaving in the
face of death—indeed, an affirmation of connection via death.
Her affirmation of connection, of the ties of kinship, between the
life-severed bodies of her kinsmen, prefigures the eventual para-
dox she embodies and exposes, and provides a reported trace of
her presence as a weaver of *différance*. As she gives the command
to burn her brother and son on the same pyre, she is identified by
name; a few lines later, she has become a woman mourning (*Ides
gnornode*, 1117), identifiable with the anonymous woman who
mourns Beowulf's death. Following the second round of hostility,
the poet concludes the song with a reference to Hildeburh, now a
nameless queen among a list of war trophies, all "ferried" (*feredon*,
1154, 1158) back to Denmark. But this time it is a completely
passive image; we watch her as she is moved across the chess-
board, given, and then taken. She has become an object, like the
precious swords and cups elsewhere in the poem. Like these
objects, she too is ambiguous, translated into the chain of signifi-
cation as an emblem of both death and victory, but the woman has
disappeared:

Ða wæs heal roden
feonda feorum,   swilce Fin slægen,
cyning on corþre,   ond seo cwen numen.
Sceotend Scyldinga   to scypon feredon
eal ingesteald   eorðcyninges,
swylce hie æt Finnes ham   findan meahton
sigla searogimma.   Hie on sælade
drihtlice wif   to Denum feredon,
læddon to leodum.   (1151–59)

(Then the hall was stained with the life-blood of enemies, likewise
Finn was slain, the king among his troop, and his queen taken.
Scylding warriors brought to the ships all the house possessions of
the king of the land, such jewels and treasures as they could find in
Finn's home. They brought the noble woman on a sea-journey to the
Danes, led her back to her people.)

To her people? Who, or what, are they? Has the poet not just
described the annihilation of everyone that this woman has any
connection with? We know that Hildeburh has nowhere to go, no
space or place to be. The poet's story has, in effect, chronicled the
stages of her complete disappearance. She has become the fig-
urehead Helen, whose war is waged "for-her and without-her." If
silence may be said to resound, that is what happens at the end of
this story. The idea or the image of Hildeburh exists only through
our apprehension of her absence, who she is or was is discernible
only as an echo or a "trace," which continually effaces itself. The
silence at the end of her story is that of a kind of paralysis of
understanding, a momentary point of standoff when the play of
paradox is revealed. It is an uncomfortable silence for the reader
(perhaps also for the Anglo-Saxon hearer), a silence that argues
persuasively for permission for the other, that demands recogni-
tion of the "other" as brother or son or husband, as the closest of
kin.

    The trace of Hildeburh does not lurk passively, as the vision of a
failed peace-weaver impotently spinning and enmeshed in her
own web of paradox. The silence she creates affronts, forces a
confrontation with unresolvable ambiguity, *declares* paradox. This
woman weaver, unlike the weaver in Freud's construct who weaves
out of shame to conceal her own lack, makes present the trace of
the absence that is imposed upon her: *she images the lack that is
defining her.* Her silence is actively experienced as an other desire
that momentarily collapses the ever-forward momentum toward

death of dominant desire; she serves other forms of movement and potential as she embodies and enacts the web of *différance*.

The Voice of Wealhtheow: Peace-Weaver in a Double Bind

Immediately following Hildeburh's silence we hear the voice of Wealhtheow, the only woman in the poem who actually speaks. It is initially tempting to set up a clear parallel between these two women: what one does with silence, the other does with words; both are hysterics who challenge the violent, death-centered, symbolic order that systematically negates them as women, queens, wives, or mothers. The fact that Wealhtheow uses language, however, necessarily adds another dimension of ambiguity to the hysteric's already complex function. She, like Hildeburh, simultaneously enacts and embodies *différance*, but as a weaver who also uses words, she adds yet another layering to the play of difference. Moreover, in her attempt to use language against violence, Wealhtheow stands at one of the poem's most important crossroads, embodying the problematic dialectic of a major social transition.

As a nonsignifying participant in both the masculine social order and the symbolic order of language, Wealhtheow's double negation engages not only the problematic of self, and of the feminine, but also that of language in the poem. Before looking at the queen's specific use of words, I want to examine briefly the context that engenders them and look at the poem's general relation to language. The world of *Beowulf* is poised between language and violence as systems of representation. Following Paul Ricoeur, we can posit language initially and simplistically as the opposite of violence, as a means of both understanding and controlling violence: "It is for a being who speaks, who in speaking pursues meaning, who has already entered the discussion and who knows something about rationality that violence is or becomes a problem. Thus violence has its meaning in its other: language. And the same is true reciprocally. Speech, discussion, and rationality also draw their unit of meaning from the fact that they are an attempt to reduce violence" (1974: 89).

On this level, the poem continually examines the efficacy of language, especially the making, breaking, and keeping of oaths, which are the means of developing cultural memory through words. Language provides a different means of remembrance, replacing the function of violence, cruelty, and spectacle, which, according to Nietzsche, forge memory in a barbaric society: "there is perhaps nothing more terrible in man's earliest history than his mnemotechnics. . . . Whenever man has thought it necessary to create a memory for himself, his effort has been attended with torture, blood, sacrifice" (192–93).

While *Beowulf* does not contain some of the extremes that Nietzsche cites as examples (castration, murder of firstborn), there are many reminders in the poem of the ongoing link between violence and signification. We are never far from what Deleuze and Guattari, in their development of Nietzsche's discussion, call the "inscription in the flesh." Coexisting with the speech of the poem are literal signs: Grendel's claw wrenched from its socket and nailed to the gables of Heorot; his head severed from his dead body by Beowulf and dragged by four men back to Hrothgar's hall; Aeschere's head displayed on the path to Grendel's mere; everywhere a pileup of bodies, nameless victims and famous heroes; funeral pyres consuming the dead. The poem embodies both literal and representational orders of significiation; chapter 2 examined this coexistence of barbaric and imperial sign-orders as a continual crisscrossing of temporal-spatial values, where the physical world subsumes the mental and vice versa, and where the linguistic sign thereby developed its peculiar density, resonance, and kinetic power.

The poem's blend of the literal and representational has often been examined in terms of religious transition, as the movement from paganism to Christianity. That Hrothgar and the Danes may revert to heathen practices in troubled times and also thank God for deliverance via Beowulf is just one instance of such blending, which has caused considerable critical debate about where exactly the poem stands. I have emphasized throughout that positing the telos of transition is less appropriate to *Beowulf* than the attempt to maintain the irresolution of either the metonymic mode of its language or of the dynamic and expansive interaction of its signs. The poem requires that we maintain a kind of double vision.

Consider, for example, some well-known words in the poem, which blend the literal and representational within language. The conclusion of Hrothgar's famous "sermon" to Beowulf, one of the most analyzed and sophisticated examples of speech in Old English poetry as a whole, offers thanks to God for the gory sight of Grendel's head:

> Þæs sig Metode þanc,
> ecean Dryhtne,   þæs ðe ic on aldre gebad,
> þæt ic on þone hafelan   heorodreorigne
> ofer eald gewin   eagum starige!   (1778–81)

(Thanks be to God, eternal Lord, that I have lived to see, that after long-standing strife I might stare with my own eyes on that blood-stained head.)

Within this most "civilized" of linguistic representations in the poem, we see that inscription in the flesh remains very much alive as a form of signification.

Deleuze and Guattari maintain that these literal signs do not betoken "some ill-defined or natural violence that might be commissioned to explain the history of mankind; cruelty is the movement of culture that is realized in bodies and inscribed on them"; and, moreover, reiterating Ricoeur's point, "it is this cruel system of inscribed signs that renders man capable of language, and gives him a memory of the spoken word" (145). This memory comes and goes in *Beowulf*; or, more accurately, the poem's capacity for inter- or cross-signification, the interchangeability of words, deeds, and things that I have described in chapter 2, makes for a fluid boundary between speech and act.

This fluidity, this coexistence of literal and representational sign-orders, of violence and language, forms part of the context of language use in general in the poem, and of female language use in particular. In the masculine, heroic mode, words must translate into actions, the hero's spoken boast achieves signification only in literal, or bodily, inscription. Elsewhere, in the masculine economy of the poem, we see the tenuous hold of language, of oaths sworn, exploded by memory—perhaps in the visual shape of an ancestral sword—of past violence. To break or rearrange this chain of signification, words must entirely substitute for deeds, not merely translate them, and this is one of the ways in which Wealhtheow's words differ from others in the poem. The attempt to move from inscription in the flesh to inscription in language, from bodily to verbal representation, is best demonstrated by the words of this woman, which we hear in a dual context, from within and without the masculine economy. Wealhtheow's speeches are, at this initial level of my discussion of language, an exhortation to warriors to remember their words, a plea for language to prevail, to replace its opposite, violence.

"This formal opposition," Ricoeur goes on to state, "does not exhaust the problem, but only encircles with a thick line surrounding emptiness" (1974: 90). We can abstract the idea of discourse and oppose it to violence simply enough, but language in use, language as spoken, used by speakers (and vice versa), all present another version of the initial problem of violence. That language itself may be a highly systemized form of violence is now a familiar critical assumption. Foucault maintains that the movement from literal to representational inscription is neither forward nor progressive: "Humanity does not gradually progress from combat to combat until it arrives at universal reciprocity, where the rule of law finally replaces warfare; humanity installs each of its violences in a system of rules and thus proceeds from domination to domination" (87).

Locating the queen's words within this continuum, or syndrome, of progressively generated, and institutionalized, rhetorical forms of violence is further complicated by gender. Whether language creates violence or violence creates language, de Lauretis argues that "both views of the relation between rhetoric and violence contain and indeed depend on the same representation of sexual difference" and that violence becomes "engendered" in the process of its institutionalized representation (1987: 32–33).

As we listen to Queen Wealhtheow assert the rule of language over the rule of violence, we see her own double subjugation: she is manipulated by the same rule of language that she seeks to assert, and as a speaking woman she must use and be used by the language of the masculine economy. Wealhtheow's speeches offer a demonstration of the Lacanian assumption that language is our inscription into patriarchy; language embodies the Name-of-the-Father, or phallocentric Law, and is the point at which we enter the symbolic order. In Wealhtheow's language we see violence speaking and spoken against.

The queen's language is particularly interesting because of the variety of ambiguities it causes to surface—all of which make her a formidable hysteric. As a spokeswoman for the power of language, she directs desire away from literal death and speaks for desire as representation, offering, affirming ambiguity by the rejection of resolution inherent in language. As a female speaker, she is simultaneously anomalous and assimilated by, subject to the masculine order of language. There is also the possibility that she is creating a new possibility; as she scrambles the circuits of language she may be speaking herself, "against the other and against men's grammar" (Cixous and Clément, 95). To take language and turn it on its head is the only way, according to Cixous and Clément, that the woman speaker may "blow up the Law" (95).

The complexity of Queen Wealhtheow's character and her function in the poem—a complexity that begins with the ambiguous connotations of her name itself—have met with a variety of critical responses, all of which have been well chronicled by Damico.[17] But, as I have pointed out earlier, these often result in a reductive either/or assessment. She is either a type of victim, whether tragic or ironic; an antitype of Grendel's monstrous mother and therefore understood through opposition. More recently Damico casts her as an actively powerful valkyrie figure, who nonetheless has been bifurcated into two personalities. The queen represents the more acceptable, less overtly violent, attributes of the valkyrie, while the poet "follows the customary portrayal of the valkyrie as a deadly battle-demon in his characterization of Grendel's mother" (Damico, 46). The division of attributes is a means of dissipating the menace and ambivalence of these "sublime noblewomen" with whom Damico ranks Wealhtheow; a Christian poet, she points out, would have to handle the valkyrie figure with care (53). It may not be necessary, or even appropriate, however, to make a choice between these extremes, to define Wealhtheow by means of oppositions that she both encompasses and resists; instead, we can try to perceive how she might define herself, glimpsing the process through the mirror of her language.

Complementing the notion that language may be seen as an attempt to control, codify, or even eliminate violence is the idea of a "speech community," a group of individuals who undertake a kind of social contract in their agreement that certain words will work in certain ways: or, in the words of J. L. Austin and John Searle, *their* saying makes it so. I am going to use the premise that language is performative to ask what actual overall relation language bears to the violent social reality of its speakers, and will borrow on occasion some terminology from speech act theory to ask what specific relation the words of the female speaker have to the reality of the speech community in *Beowulf*. I propose that there are roughly three levels on which words, or more properly speech acts, function in *Beowulf*.

The first I call the "Beowulfian" mode, the grand, simple, and often devastating equation of words with reality, where intention or boast is tantamount to deed or actuality: saying will indeed make it so. Beowulf forms a speech community of one, however; he is judge and jury. His heroism demands a degree of self-absorption that closes the social circuit of language; he creates his separate relation to reality.[18]

The second level is more mundane, more attached to the world of personal and social interaction: words of greeting, explaining, expressing gratitude or emotion, words of daily communication. (Beowulf is quite capable of using words in these ways as well.) Oaths and promises and marriage vows fall into this category also, although they represent more serious, public versions of commitment to an agreed-upon code of social interaction.

The third level on which speech acts function, which is my present concern, is a form of opposite of the first: a level of failure where language is subsumed, overtaken by action, where violence breaks the linguistic social contract, where the connection of language to reality is shown to be tenuous, fragile, and fraught with complexity. This is also the level at which desire as representation provides the initiation into ambiguity, and forces an acknowledgment of the violent potential of language. There are few "speakers" at this level in the poem. Hildeburh belongs here, a mute witness to the failure of marriage vows and oaths of peace. At this level we might also place the wordless sorrowing noise, a garbled parody of language, produced by the female mourners of the poem—Grendel's less-than-human mother included. The primary speaker for this third level is Queen Wealhtheow, who makes two formal, public speeches at the banquet in honor of Beowulf's first victory. These speeches, it is important to remember, follow immediately upon the "entertainment" of the story of Finn and Hildeburh: one queen takes up in language what the other had left in silence.

The Queen's first speech is addressed to her husband, in the presence of her two sons, Hrethric and Hrothmund, the visiting hero who is sitting next to them, her nephew Hrothulf, and the entire Danish court. The second is an equally public address to Beowulf. Dividing the speeches is the story of the valuable neck-ring that she gives to Beowulf, an account of its past and a depressing glimpse into its future, when it will be worn by Hygelac on his death raid. I quote both speeches in full in order to

examine the succession of ideas and the success or otherwise of
her words as speech acts:

'Onfoh þissum fulle,   freodrihten min,
sinces brytta!   Þu nu on sælum wes,
goldwine gumena,   ond to Geatum spræc
mildum wordum,   swa sceal man don!
Beo wið Geatas glæd,   geofena gemyndig,
nean ond feorran   þu nu hafast.
Me man sægde,   þæt þu for sunu wolde
hererinc habban.   Heorot is gefælsod,
beahsele beorhta;   bruc þenden þu mote
manigra medo,   ond þinum læf
folc ond rice   þonne ðu forð scyle,
metodsceaft seon.   Ic minne can
glædne Hroþulf,   þæt he þa geoguðe wile
arum healdan,   gyf þu ær þonne he,
wine Scildinga,   worold oflætest;
wene ic þæt he mid gode   gyldan wille
uncran eaferan,   gif he þæt eal gemon,
hwæt wit to willan   ond to wordmyndum
umborwesendum ær   arna gefremedon.'   (1169–87)

("Accept this cup, my dear lord, giver of treasure! Be happy now,
goldfriend of men, and to the Geats speak with kind words, as a man
should do! Be gracious to the Geats, mindful of gifts that you now
possess from near and far. I have heard that you would have this
warrior for a son. Heorot, bright ring-hall, is cleansed; make use of
many rewards while you can, and to your own sons leave folk and
kingdom, when you shall go forth to see death. I know my gracious
Hrothulf, that he will hold these youths in honor, if you, friend of the
Scyldings, forsake this world before he does; I expect that he will
repay our sons with goodness, if he remembers all the kindnesses we
performed for his pleasure and honor when he was growing up.")

'Bruc þisses beages,   Beowulf leofa,
hyse, mid hæle,   ond þisses hrægles neot,
þeodgestreona,   ond geþeoh tela,
cen þec mid cræfte,   ond þyssum cnyhtum wes
lara liðe!   Ic þe þæs lean geman.
Hafast þu gefered,   þæt ðe feor ond neah
ealne wideferhþ   weras ehtigað,
efne swa side   swa sæ bebugeð,
windgeard, weallas,   Wes þenden þu lifige,
aeþeling, eadig!   Ic þe an tela

sincgestreona.   Beo þu suna minum
dædum gedefe,   dreamhealdende!
Her is æghwylc eorl   oþrum getrywe,
modes milde,   mandrihtne hold,
þegnas syndon geþwære,   þeod ealgearo,
druncne dryhtguman   doð swa ic bidde.'   (1216–31)

("Enjoy this neck-ring with safety, Beowulf, beloved youth, and make use of this corselet, of our people's treasure; prosper well, declare yourself with strength, and be kind of counsel to these youths. I shall remember to reward you for that. You have brought it about that men shall praise you from far and near for a long time to come, even as far as the sea, home of the winds, encompasses the walls of the shore. Be blessed, prince, while you live. I wish you well of your treasure. Be kind in deeds to my sons, happy man. Here every nobleman is true to the other, mild of heart, loyal to his lord; the thanes are united, the people willing; the wine-drinking warriors do as I bid.")

Both speeches offer a dense array of contradictions. In "The Voice of Beowulf," Carmen Cramer argues that the queen's language is "more commanding and authoritarian, even as she displays proper and gracious feminine courtesy, than Hrothgar's. When Wealhtheow addresses her lord (1169–1185), she uses five imperatives" (43). The general tone and style of Wealhtheow's language are more reminiscent of Beowulf's: "Wealhtheow, like the active Beowulf and unlike the rather passive Hrothgar, speaks in the present and future tenses . . . only twice in her two first speeches does she talk about the past; she is a person oriented to the active present" (Cramer, 43).

While all these observations are accurate, the speech of the hero and the queen differ in at least one important respect. Despite the occasionally uncertain tone of Beowulf's last speeches, Charles McNally, in his detailed analysis of all the hero's speeches, concludes that "the speech acts the main character of the epic performs throughout are primarily those of commitment: promises, intentions, boasts, all of which he sincerely delivers and carries out" (191). With the possible exception of her promise to reward Beowulf (1220), Wealhtheow's language is noticeably devoid of commissives, "those illocutionary acts whose point is to commit the speaker (again in some varying degrees) to some future course of action" (Searle, 11). It would overstep the poem's bounds of congruity and possibility for a female speaker to commit an

essentially nonexistent self—one outside the chain of significa-
tion—to a course of action. For the most part, she tries to get
others to do things, or represents the conditions of her world as
she observes them, not as she creates them. In language, as
elsewhere in the poem, she must be translated into the terms of
the masculine economy; obliged to speak herself through others,
she must choose different varieties of speech acts.

In his analysis of the illocutionary point of all speech acts,[19]
Searle introduces the dimension of "direction of fit," whether the
speaker is trying to match the world to words or words to world,
and the notion that the sincerity condition of any speech act must
be located along a spectrum of psychological states; both concepts
are useful in mapping out the complexity and ambiguity of the
queen's speeches. When Wealhtheow uses directives (speech acts
which try to move others to do something),[20] which she does a
great deal, we have the difficult task of assessing where to place
her along a spectrum ranging from pleading to commanding, and
just how assured or desperate is the desire to make the world
match her words.

Wealhtheow begins her first speech by telling the king, in
imperative form, to accept the cup from her and rejoice in his
present happiness, but then attempts to undo her husband's past
words by a kind of public admonition or embarrassment. Her
exhortation to the king to do what is proper calls attention to his
previous impropriety: his excessively generous offer to adopt
Beowulf as his son when he already has two of his own. The
public, ceremonial context of her words is a reminder of the power
of the linguistic social contract and the law it upholds, and by her
measured words she seeks to negate her husband's rash promise.

In the first part of her speech to Beowulf, Wealhtheow also
makes skillful use of the ceremonial context, and her own formal
role as cupbearer and treasure dispenser, to extract a promise
from the hero, summoning ritual to the aid of language. In her
address to both husband and hero, she subjugates objects—
drinking cup and treasures—to the rule of language. She tries to
translate and confine their function to the representative domain
of language, arrogating their previous translatability into literal
signification. Indeed this cup-bearing scene may be visualized as
a wonderfully complex enactment and embodiment of the weav-
ing of *différance*. As the peace-weaver who is herself the represen-
tation and embodiment of her function, Wealhtheow physically

draws lines of connection, enacts the process of weaving, as she carries the cup from one warrior to another. This literal and representational weaving resonates in her language, where the play of her own absence and presence continues to present, to represent, the echo or trace of her presence.

This woman speaker trespasses in language as she is also trespassing in the masculine warrior stronghold of the hall—the "natural" invades the "cultural," or the women's world of the hut intrudes into the masculine domain of the hall in Earl's Freudian terms (1983: 150)—but only to turn this opposition into paradox. Her presence, her actions, and her words betoken connection, but at the same time they diagram an ongoing dialectic of separation and connection. The weaver, the activity of weaving, and the web itself whirl incessantly in and out of focus in the play of levels of representation and layers of inconclusive, unresolvable ambiguity.

But I am getting ahead of myself here in anticipating the total ambiguity of her words; let me return to specific levels of its operation. Her persistent use of the imperative in the first part of both speeches appears to assert the rule of language. The formal or ceremonial directive, "accept this cup," is paralleled to her directive to her husband to do what a man should do, to use kind—and appropriate—words to the Geats, and then to do what perhaps should appear obvious: leave the kingdom to its rightful inheritors. When she rewards the hero with ceremonial propriety, she aligns and publicly identifies the gifts of treasure with a future commitment on Beowulf's part to her young sons. This identification is further cemented by the one commissive Wealhtheow uses; she tells Beowulf that she will reward him in the future, asserting her power to do, to act, in the only way appropriate or permitted to her. The queen uses all the kinds of ammunition, actual and representational, that she has. Her language parallels, assumes ritual. But is the queen pleading or commanding? At what point does she believe the world will match her words, or even that language itself will control the violence that continually threatens her world?

Her imperative directives to enjoy and be happy are accompanied in both speeches by a conditional "while you now possess" (1174), "while you can" (1177), or "while you live" (1224), generating a free-floating temporal precariousness easily applicable to both the queen and her audience. Whether Wealhtheow is rather assuredly and urbanely reminding both the old king and the young hero of their mortality, or whether she is "a very worried mother in a very fragile world" (Renoir, 1975: 229), is difficult to determine. What the queen may or may not believe is entirely a matter of opinion. Her observations of her world are expressed in representatives, speech acts that "commit the speaker (in varying degrees) to something's being the case, to the truth of the expressed proposition" (Searle, 10). Representatives also necessarily involve difficult and subtle decisions about sincerity conditions and psychological state, as Searle makes clear:

The direction of fit is words to the world; the psychological state expressed is Belief (that p). It is important to emphasize that words such as "belief" and "commit" are here intended to mark dimensions. . . . Thus there is a difference between *suggesting* that p or *putting it forward as a hypothesis* that p on the one hand and *insisting* that p or *solemnly swearing* that p on the other. The degree of belief and commitment may approach or even reach zero. . . . The simplest test of a representative is this: can you literally characterize it (*inter alia*) as true or false. (10–11)

When the queen says that she knows her nephew will treat her sons well if their father dies before him, is she representing what she believes to be the truth? What is her degree of commitment to her own words, to the effective power of the language she wields against the violence that always seems to be imminent?

Analyzing the truth value of representatives is to some degree another way of talking about irony. The audience already knows, because the poet has already told them, that bad faith between Hrothulf and Hrothgar will erupt in the future (1018–19). Also, we know very early in the poem that Hrothgar's great hall is destined to be burned down as a result of the Danish-Heathobard feud that Hrothgar is trying to patch up by using his daughter as a peace-weaver (81–85). But the queen does not have this overview. One could claim that the plain reality of reasonable expectation would undercut considerably the truth value of her statement regarding her nephew: "anyone who does not hear anxiety in Wealhtheow's speech about Hrothulf will act towards her offspring," Robinson insists, "must think that Mark Antony genuinely believes Caesar's murderers to be honorable men" (1984: 109). The audience and the queen would be foolish and naive not to expect the worst. The story of Hildeburh is no mere parable, but a fact of life. The tenuous hold of language is well attested to in the world of the poem, and in the queen's context especially. As she represents her view of her nephew and his future actions, the direction of fit becomes problematic; the simply representative coexists in tension with its opposite; these words are also an attempt to organize the world to match *them,* and the sincerity condition of belief is necessarily attenuated.

A similar situation arises at the end of her second speech, when Wealhtheow represents her view of the harmony of the Danish court. Is she insisting, hypothesizing, or using a representative to express a covert directive—that is, lying? Damico asserts that "the queen states unambiguously that the warriors in the hall pay her homage and obedience" (6), rejecting the possibility of dramatic or tragic irony in this speech.[21] Military power is consistent with an autonomous warrior-woman image, which Damico argues is an important facet of Wealhtheow's compound personality as a valkyrie figure. Damico interprets the queen's words as authoritative and literal.[22] Others read this part of the speech quite differently. Given the poetic tradition of women as passive, suffering victims, "one may surely be excused for detecting the hint of a pathetic ring in her attempt at clinching her request [to Beowulf] with the assertion that the warriors in the hall always do her bidding" (Renoir, 1975: 230).

It may be impossible to determine the truth value of these representations, or what the queen actually believes. Larry M. Sklute thinks that her words are important and influential but somehow out of her control, because "she herself may not realize fully the implications of her admonitions" (540). Kliman does not even identify the woman with the words; she characterizes both of the queen's speeches as a series of "disjointed statements unconnected to any request or demand of her own" (34). Kliman also suggests that "the argument by juxtaposition leaves the connections to be made by her husband" (34). Returning to the argument of chapter 1, however, we could also postulate that the unresolved contiguous association of the metonymic mode is an open-ended process, leaving meaning construction to the reader and always *in* process. Instead of trying to figure the queen out, or to pin her down, perhaps it is more useful to evaluate her words as an affirmation of the rule of representation. She is claiming the attention and invoking the rules of her speech community, holding up for public inspection the linguistic promises that the community has made to itself.

The domain of representation, however, opens up, even ne-
cessitates, a multitude of possibilities; in affirming the rule of
language, Wealhtheow also affirms ambiguity and escapes defi-
nition. The queen may be a consummate politician, able to mani-
pulate her husband and Beowulf with her verbal skill, engaging
language to do the work of coercion and therefore coopted by the
masculine economy; she may be a desperate woman afraid for
herself and her children, naively using words to stave off violence;
she may be a dignified, self-confident noblewoman who believes
in the civilizing, ordering power of language, unaware of its
violent potential; she may be a polite, proper, and ineffectual
ornamental addition to the poem, whose verbal power is merely
ceremonial; she may be a military force in her own right with the
actual power to back up her words, whose language is thinly
veiled violence. She may have more in common with Grendel's
monstrous, unwomanly, and overtly violent mother than with the
feminine ideal of peace-loving peace-weaver. She may be seen as
controlling or controlled by her words, a fly netted in the amber of
her own language. Or perhaps there is no connection between the
language she uses and who she is, and the multiple personalities
suggested by her language are a means of escaping and resisting
definition, of deflecting binary categorization.

When she falls silent, we are stranded unceremoniously on the
complex, thoroughly ambiguous, shores of language. We hear a
kind of formless babble, the antiphon to Hildeburh's silence. As
Hildeburh reveals the trace of self through silence and absence,
Wealhtheow may be glimpsed through the mirror of language.
But her image, like Hildeburh's, never resolves into clear black and
white; it can only be apprehended through paradox. Wealhtheow,
despite her eloquent speech, does not speak herself, neither does
she "blow up the Law." Her role as hysteric calls language into
question, subjects it to examination: this woman speaker, who is
as absent from language as she is from the masculine symbolic
order, temporarily introduces herself as female subject into the
order of language, and her words, like no others in the poem, strip
bare the paradoxical core of the whole linguistic project and her
relation to it.

Wealhtheow leaves us with the riddle of unresolved and unre-
solvable ambiguity; in the Peircean semeiotic terms of chapter 2,
her words spin a linguistic paradox of multipotential but essen-
tially inconclusive interpretants, disallowing clear teleological

direction and resolution. Her speech, like Hildeburh's silence and, as we shall see, Modthryth's unpredictability, is a powerful and inescapable index to ambiguity. But this is far less life-threatening than its opposite and counterpart: the death-centered mode of desire affirmed throughout the poem and especially in the words of its hero, where the illusion, albeit a conscious or chosen one in Beowulf's case, of the subject in language is translated into egocentric certainty and into yet another illusion of control. The queen offers an alternative to this death-centered, tragic morality, which "prefers the blind and lucid Oedipus at Colonnus to Oedipus the King, blind to his sins" (Cixous and Clément, 40), which elevates resolution, despite its inherently reductive and blinding aspects, over toleration of the other. Like the silent Hildeburh, Wealhtheow offers a verbal plea for permission for the other, and also a disquieting glimpse of the presence of the other in the task of interpretation demanded by her language: "Only the unsolved riddle, the process of riddle-work before its final completion, is a confrontation with otherness" (Gallop, 1982: 61).

Modthryth as Spectacle and Spectator

Modthryth, or Thryth, whose very name has proved problematic to critics, occupies a brief and much emended section of the poem.[23] Her story is "very abruptly introduced and is the most difficult of all for 'whole-hearted admirers' to justify" (Crossley-Holland, 139). Perhaps even more so than Wealhtheow, this queen's brief appearance has given rise to a critical consternation that well illustrates a binary pressure coming from without the poem, a need to define and to somehow account for her as one of the most unruly details of a variously described but nonetheless assumed whole. Critics have attempted to explain her in a wide variety of ways; some have explained her away completely, taking *modþryðo* as a noun meaning "mindstrength" or "arrogance," and not as a proper name.[24] Bloomfield comes close to dismissing her when he emphasizes the "interrupting quality" of her appearance in the poem, and sees her story and other scattered digressions in the last part of the poem as products of heroic senility. Her story is one of the references to the past that increasingly take over in the poem, which "reduplicates as far as is possible by structural means the mode of aged thinking" and generates "an atmosphere suitable to the story of an old and worn-out hero" (58). Others suggest that she is included in the poem on account of her marriage to Offa, whose Mercian descendant, Offa II, might have been flattered at the reference.[25]

She is mentioned in connection with Hygd, Hygelac's young and gracious queen, and is most often interpreted as an instance of the Beowulf-poet's technique of presenting contrasts. In order to make clear the nature and duties of the good king, Hrothgar cites the example of Heremod, who did everything wrong (1709–22). Modthryth, then, serves a similar function, operating in contrast to Queen Hygd. Adrien Bonjour rationalizes the problematic appearance of Modthryth by extending this opposition principle even further: Modthryth, who eventually reforms her behavior, and Heremod, who starts out auspiciously and then deteriorates, serve as foils for each other, and both of them are "implicitly contrasted with Offa, whose whole career was a long and continuous success and who, therefore, in the poet's brief and condensed eulogy, may give us a prefiguration of Beowulf's own future successful leadership" (1950: 55). By such a circuitous route, a place is found for the unmannerly queen in the larger context of the poem, one that connects, and assimilates her through opposition.

The figure of Modthryth herself and the notion of a possible separate or individual identity for her not dependent on binary classification have not received much critical attention. In her analysis of contemporary film narrative, de Lauretis raises a question that also sheds some light on this shadowy, ill-defined, overdefined queen. With particular reference to Hitchcock's work, she asserts that the development of suspense in film narrative, and the progress of narrative in general, always casts the question of desire in terms of "what will he do when he finds out?" (1984: 155). What effects do Modthryth's actions have, what response does she elicit, and how does she serve or thwart dominant desire in the poem—in effect, what is to be done about her? These are the kinds of questions that have been asked of her. Instead of trying to resolve the "problem" of what is to be done with her, I want to look at what *she* does when *she* "finds out," and what she does to us as readers. Her power to disturb, her "hysterical" potential, is enormous, and perhaps the more striking by virtue of the brevity of her cameo appearance.

With the notable exception of Grendel's mother, Modthryth is the most unwomanly, unqueenly female in the poem. She is vain, mean, proud, apparently gratuitously violent, aggressive, power-hungry, and initially displays an almost casual contempt for men. She is "tamed" by her marriage to Offa, transformed by the love and guidance of a good husband into a model wife and queen. In her ambiguous role as hysteric, she begins by rocking the boat, by challenging, even inverting the values of the prevailing symbolic order (much as Beowulf does when he hypothesizes the paralysis of indecision); she is then "cured" (as is Beowulf who finally chooses the "active" course of resolution, the closure of heroic binarism), a textbook example of the onetime hysteric assimilated by the familial symbolic order: "The family reassimilates her otherness, and like an amoeba, finds its single cell revitalized, stronger than before" (Gallop, 1982: 133). Modthryth causes a temporary shudder of discomfort, followed by a generalized sigh of relief that the disorder she threatens has been contained and that things are once more under the control of the masculine economy.

Her assimilation, however, requires oversimplified binary ratio-nalization: aggressive, "masculine" behavior is not a "lady/queen-like custom" (*cwenlic þeaw*, 1940), and is thus construed as a force for evil. Hansen makes this point clear: "Just as Beowulf, at the height of his career, can still control the malevolent elements in his world, so of course the wicked queen here can be subdued by the wisdom and love of her husband Offa" (115). Moreover, Mod-thryth's exceptional husband, according to Sklute, "was possessed of those rare qualities that can control women with confused libidinal drives" (536). Although categorizing Modthryth as simply evil as a result of her sexually anomalous behavior is an efficient means of superficially restoring the poem's apparent moral status quo, it cannot address the persistent ambiguity she introduces into the narrative, nor accurately account for her power and "shock value" as a hysteric. To understand this, we have only to look more carefully at *what* she does, at the specific nature of her "evil."

At the center of Modthryth's rebellion is her refusal to be looked at, to become an object, which necessarily results in her rejection of the female peace-weaver role:

> Modþryðo wæg,
> fremu folces cwen,   firen ondrysne;
> nænig þa dorste   deor geneþan

swæsra gesiđa,   nefne sinfrea,
þæt hire an dæges   eagum starede;
ac him wælbende   weotode tealde
handgewriþene;   hraþe seoþđan wæs
æfter mundgripe   mece geþinged,
þæt hit sceadenmæl   scyran moste,
cwealmbealu cyđan.   Ne biđ swylc cwenlic þeaw
idese to efnanne,   þeah đe hio ænlicu sy,
þætte freođuwebbe   feores onsæce
æfter ligetorne   leofne mannan.
Huru þæt onhohsnode   Hemminges mæg. . . .   (1931–44)

(Modthryth, excellent queen of the people, carried out a terrible
crime; there was none of the beloved followers so brave, except a great
lord, who dared venture to stare at her with his eyes in the light of
day; but he would discover appointed to him handwoven deadly
bonds; soon after the seizure it was decided by the sword, the
patterned blade would settle it, proclaiming death. That is no queen-
ly custom for a lady to perform, even though she be beautiful, that a
peace-weaver should deprive a beloved man of life on account of a
pretended insult. However, the Hemming's kinsman (Offa) put a
stop to that. . . .)

Her rebellion constitutes a direct confrontation with the mas-
culine symbolic order of the poem. Despite her beauty, Mod-
thryth will not consent to be a feminine spectacle in a masculine
arena, refusing to join the ranks of the gold-adorned queens who
circulate among the warriors as visible treasure (as does Hygd, for
example). She rejects objectification, refuses to be an *objet petit à*,
Lacan's term for the appropriated, domesticated other that the
masculine economy substitutes for the genuine, unrealizable
Other (*Autre*). By refusing to be held in the masculine "gaze,"
Modthryth underscores the connection between seeing and mas-
culinity, between the eye and the phallus, insisted on by Lacan:
"It is inasmuch as, at the heart of the experience of the uncon-
scious, we are dealing with that organ (the phallus)—determined
in the subject by the inadequacy of the castration complex—that
we can grasp to what extent the eye is caught up in a similar
dialectic" (1981: 102). Modthryth's rejection of the gaze briefly
exposes its particular oculocentric tyranny: both the illusion of
subjectivity and the privileging of the subject that attends the
apprehension of the world characterized as "I see myself seeing
myself." "The privilege of the subject," Lacan asserts, "seems to be

established here from that bipolar reflexive relation by which, as soon as I perceive, my representations belong to me" (81). Modthryth's initial refusal to be "seen" is also a refusal to participate in a self-aggrandizing mode of perception, in a *"belong to me* aspect of representations, so reminiscent of property" (Lacan, 81).[26]

Despite her dramatic rejection of a fundamental premise of the symbolic order, Modthryth does not achieve a rupture, or make a change, in that order. Indeed, the violent form of her rebellion confronts the system on its own death-centered terms. Her complicity—also a form of mimicry—in the masculine objectifying, destructive mode, however, also demonstrates her dual role as hysteric, as both heroine and victim, whose ambiguity is part of her power to disturb. Her retaliation repeats the inscription in the flesh, the poem's insistent connection between violence and signification, that Wealhtheow tries so hard to sever. Modthryth turns the masculine gaze back upon itself, briefly becoming a spectator, an overseer herself, but then is co-opted in a joint spectacle. Her violent response to being "seen" reveals the barely displaced violence of the act of staring; she calls attention to, even makes a spectacle of, that same connection between violence and signification in which she also participates. She succeeds in making a spectacle of herself and of the masculine economy; her dramatic rearrangement, via inversion and restoration, of the spectator/spectacle, or passive/active binary dynamic, resists complacent resolution and affirms ambiguity; in spite of her reformed wifely personality, she remains a discomfiting presence.

Modthryth causes further disturbance from the point of view of motivation. Unlike the other overtly violent female in the poem, Grendel's mother, Modthryth does not appear to have a familial motivation. Although Chance and Damico find the closest parallels for her behavior in the masculine aggression of Grendel's mother,[27] even such alien monstrous proclivities find their rationalization in the familiar and familial vengeance code that pervades the poem. Modthryth is not out there engaging in confrontation, as Grendel's mother does with actions, as Wealhtheow does with words, on account of someone else; she is nobody's mother. Her display of violence and her use of power are self-generated. She spurns male attention as vehemently as those chaste, aggressive female saints and martyrs, but not in the name of Christ. Her rebellion comes from no recognizable source or place, just as her story surfaces in the poem with no immediately apparent connection to the main narrative. She utterly rejects a hypothetical "identity" as a peace-weaver: instead she actively weaves the "deadly bonds" of death. Modthryth's behavior and motivation are not identifiable or explicable, unless we accept the poet's explanation that it is all in her head—an imaginary insult, pretended injury—or agree with Renoir that she is "so far gone on the unhappy path of paranoiac delusions" (1975: 230) that she cannot function properly. We might also entertain Sklute's suggestion that she suffers from "confused libidinal drives." Interestingly and appropriately, all these viewpoints fits the portrait of the classical hysteric.

As neither noblewoman nor monsterwoman, Modthryth escapes all definition offered by the poem; she is truly mysterious, eventually unthinkable,[28] qualities she shares with the silent, absent Hildeburh. Unlike Hildeburh, who leaves behind her profound silence and a glimpse of paradox through paralysis, we perceive the trace of Modthryth through the turmoil and upheaval she herself causes, and through the apparent narrative relief, in the form of good Queen Hygd's entrance, when she exits the poem. But my point is that she does not go away; even though she may appear to have been assimilated back into the family, the disturbance she brings to the poem does not subside with her quiescent marriage; nor is her disconcerting ghost laid to rest by her more comforting counterpart, Hygelac's young queen. She does not go away, precisely because she remains a mystery, because she escapes, however briefly, the trap of binary definition.

Modthryth offers a variation on Hildeburh's silent declaration of paradox; she reveals the trace of something that we know cannot exist in the world of the poem: the trace of a woman signifying in her own right. Her initial gesture is strikingly alien, incomprehensible, until translated into the binary language of the masculine economy. Heremod and Beowulf as antitypes operate well within binary strictures; as good or evil as they are, they still speak the same language, as it were; one idea is comprehensible, indeed manageable, in terms of the other. But the Modthryth-Hygd opposition is slightly asymmetric; there is a part of Modthryth that will not translate or match up, and this, by the process of association so endemic to this poem, must reflect on Hygd, on the young Freawaru, on all the human females in the poem. I am not suggesting that Modthryth's response is one that substantially undermines or calls into overt question the prevailing symbolic order; what I am suggesting is that she intrudes herself briefly into the poem's chain of signification, introduces dis-ease, a thrill of disgust perhaps, a tremor of amazement at the unknown. The jolt in the narrative that she provides is just enough to make us think, as we watch the gracious temperate Hygd obediently performing her womanly duties, that one never knows. . . .

Afterword

If Modthryth remains mysterious and unexpressible, Hildeburh absent and silent, and Wealhtheow profoundly ambiguous, where does this ongoing lack of definition leave these women, or where does it lead the reader? I have already stated that these chapters will come to no formal conclusion, and that this is not a book about what *Beowulf* means, but a study of the process of meaning construction from within and without the poem. In each chapter I have insisted on the idea of process, of open-ended, ongoing movement, as the controlling mode of the poem and of its interpretation. What I propose in these final remarks is not to conclude therefore, but to continue the activity of weaving: to gather up some strands of my previous discussions, to reconfigure the elements of some recurrent questions, to anticipate some emerging questions, and to trace some new lines of connection.

I began with the premise that the Old English poetic text demands a critical strategy, or variety of strategies, consonant with the terms of its difference, and that the insights of contemporary theory might embrace and revalue that difference. *Beowulf* is one of many Old English texts that offer an exemplary demonstration of the process of deconstruction, from within and without the text; but we could also state that this is simply a new term for what Anglo-Saxonists have known and studied for many years. *Beowulf* is a text of many parts that lies in parts. The convolutions, complexities, and fragmentations of the text, moreover, are matched by the history of the *Beowulf* manuscript itself, and of its interpreters and interpretations. Likewise, we can say that we already knew that Modthryth was unpredictable, or that the language of *Beowulf* is agrammatical and fragmented on many levels, and we already have our standard list of the characteristics of Old English poetry to describe and account for its metonymic quality. What is at issue here is the process of renaming, and in that process some familiar critical issues are reexamined, rewritten, and potentially transformed, while others are created, brought into language, realized for the first time. What I have been attempting to reexamine and rewrite by this ongoing process of renaming is the connection between the modern self and this ancient text, the space between language and experience, the place between words and things, and as a result the emerging issue of the interface or interplay of our own desire with that of the text comes insistently into language. What kind of *Beowulf* have we created and why? The first part of this question has been far more accessible to historical description than the second. Anglo-Saxonists *like* parts, they embrace details—the lost letter, the missing half-line, the scribal error, the elusive allusion, the questionable date—but have also succumbed to the temptations of inventing via emendation, supplying the absent details, and organizing the parts into variously described and motivated wholes. Even when the text has not been subjected to mandatory unification, some details or parts have been privileged over others and judged to be more or less "central" to the poem.

The critical activity of configuring and reconfiguring of elements of the poem has received more attention than the motivations for that activity. Tolkien raised the issue of the disjunctive relationship between the poem and its critics in 1936 when he wrote that "it has been said of *Beowulf* that its weakness lies in placing the unimportant things at the centre and the important on the outer edges. . . . I think it profoundly untrue of the poem, but strikingly true of the literature about it" (52). Tolkien identifies the questions of centrality and marginality, and the varieties of interpretational mismatches between the operations of the critic and those of the poem, but does not connect these questions to the operations of desire. In the linguistic and semiotic arguments of chapters 1 and 2 I too have skirted this issue to some extent in an attempt to focus more squarely on parts and details, and their discrete value and effect. I have not taken on the further task implicit in these arguments of describing the nature of the self "spoken" or created by a metonymically based language, or the nature of the self-sign that produces and is produced by its collaboration with the text.

Inasmuch as I have argued for an approach-in-process to desire *as* interpretation instead of the controlling, defining impulse of desire *for* interpretation, I have also restricted my examination of desire in the gender argument of chapter 3 to its operation within the text. In doing so I have been aware of both the arbitrariness and difficulty of separating the desires of text and reader, and the inevitable operation of my own desire as reader. In identifying the constructs of metonymy, dynamic semeiosis, or the operations of socially contextualized, "engendered," desire within the text with the mode of the poem, I have also identified the kind of *Beowulf* I want.

Let us follow this line of reasoning for a moment. If this open-ended text, whose difference I claim mirrors the positivity of potential rather than the negativity of deferral of meaning, is produced by my own desire, where does that take us and what kinds of new questions are brought into language as a consequence? As the continuity and irresolution of metonymy may be identified with feminine forms of desire, is one a condition for the other? When I read this poem, Beowulf's story of Hrethel with its agonizing ambivalence always exerts a tremendous pull; so, too, does the unsettled and unsettling Modthryth. Do these particularly ambiguous and unresolved parts of the poem match, or express, then, a feminine desire? If a feminist, psychoanalytic approach privileges parts and details over wholes, how might this reinscribe the detail in *Beowulf*?

Modthryth and Scyld Scefing are details; the difference has been that Scyld is considered "central" to the theme of the poem, whereas Modthryth is peripheral at best, a muffled and incoherent voice from the margins of the poem's discourse. Suppose we move this hysterical, ambivalent queen closer to the "center," or privilege Hildeburh's absence over Beowulf's illusion of presence? Do these questions simply replace the imposition of masculine unitary desire with the imposition of feminine fragmentary desire upon a long-suffering, reader-produced text, or do they bring to language issues hitherto unexpressed? My answer to this last question is an unqualified and self-conscious "both." In posing either/or questions, I am setting up binary oppositions, which I also hope to dismantle. As I have argued in the preceding chapter, what desire produces and what produces desire are inextricably interwoven, one is a function of the other, in continual dialectic with the other.

I have also discussed ways in which the notion of process, of the ongoing production and construction of meaning, engages some of the basic preoccupations of both feminist and deconstructive criticism. The many and various parts of *Beowulf*—the very stuff of deconstruction and difference—have been historically molded into wholes, made to comply with a variety of unitary motivations; it is a profoundly masculine poem enacting and depicting masculine desire from both within and without; and if the poem has assumed different shapes, these must be understood as nondefinitive configurations of interactions of external and internal desire. But this poem, like many other Old English texts, also contains all the gaps, silences, paradoxes, questions, and interventions of marginal desire—all of which are central to feminist critical inquiry. At the core of my attempt to rename contexts for the evaluation and interpretation of *Beowulf* is the revaluing of difference, a project that is both deconstructionist and feminist. Feminists, however, have questioned how far the deconstructionist concept of difference can dismantle the fundamentally paired opposition of male/female, and how the nonclosure of the continual play of elements can address the problem of identity, of constructing a means to express the inexpressible—that which remains inarticulated by Western, patriarchal and rationalist schemes of knowledge.

Jardine reminds us that, "there is, after all, a difference between really attempting to think differently and thinking the Same through the manipulation of difference" (17). The necessary stance of feminism must, then, be the consciousness of being at once in and out of ideology (de Lauretis, 1987: 10). Confronted with the difficulties of unresolved difference and her own absence, there are several possibilities for the feminist critic: "a renewed silence, a form of religion (from mysticism to political orthodoxy), or a continual attention—historical, ideological, and affective—to the place from which we speak" (Jardine, 32). This latter choice will continually engage both the reader's desire and how it is produced as ongoing elements in the construction of meaning. The web of *différance* becomes "engendered" within and without the text.

When I construct an argument for the women of *Beowulf* as deflecting or redirecting masculine desire, for example, I am aware that I am operating from within the same binary framework that I seek to dismantle. Although I might also argue that such female hysterical characteristics may be shared by marginal monsters and mainline heroes, it could be said that I have simply set up another opposition, that of death-centered masculine desire versus female as life-giver, and ranked my pair according to ideological preference. This will obviously be the case to some extent, but I am also probing the possibilities of asymmetry and dialectic. One side of the opposition we know well, the other is relatively unexplored.

Let me invoke the unsettling presence of Modthryth once more, and ask what might happen to the notion of a center if we bring her in from the margin and move her closer to it? I have argued that this queen's power resides in paradox, in her ability to elude and foil binary categorization. She embodies an impossible dialectic, one that will continually generate new configurations of oppositional elements while at the same time introducing an asymmetrical potential. Such a view of Modthryth engages the question of desire from within and without the text, and suggests how new questions might be brought to language by the conscious examination of the interplay of our own desire with that of the text.

Curiously but perhaps appropriately, this difficult queen has come to represent both the perils of overdefinition and the unpredictable yet regenerative power of process. Perhaps it is fitting to conclude, then, with Modthryth, one of the least conclusive elements in the poem, as an affirmation of process in interpretation, and to look forward to the inscription of the reader's desire in that process. The *différance* of the Old English poetic text will acquire more meaning, or in Peircean terms it will undergo the expansion and ever-increasing clarification of semeiosis, as we participate more fully in its operation and identify our selves with it, as we extend the activity of weaving to include the acknowledgment, description, and analysis of the reader's desire in continual and collaborative conjunction with that of the text. Such an attempt to include the reader has yet to be made in criticism of *Beowulf,* or of Old English poetry as a whole, but I think that this area of critical inquiry can raise new and exciting questions about the poems, and that it will open up some new dimensions of critical investigation in which the difference of this remarkable body of poetry might be engaged, valued, and enjoyed.

NOTES
BIBLIOGRAPHY
INDEX

Notes

Introduction

1. The essays by Frantzen and Venegoni, and Irvine, both appear in *Style* vol. 20., no. 2 (1986), which is devoted to a collection of articles engaging theory, primarily semiotic, and medieval studies. Other journals have similarly responded to medievalists' developing interest in theory. All volumes of *Semiotics* since 1984 contain a separate section on medieval narrative and sign theory, and the 1987 volume of *Semiotica* is a special medieval studies issue. See also *Medieval Texts and Contemporary Readers*, ed. Laurie A. Finke and Martin B. Schictman (Ithaca: Cornell University Press, 1987) for a variety of contemporary theoretical approaches to medieval texts; Finke and Schichtman's "Introduction: Critical Theory and the Study of the Middle Ages" (1–11) provides an overview of the progress of resistance to, and acceptance of, theory, which will be of interest to Anglo-Saxonists as well as medievalists in general.

Chapter 1. Language

1. All references to *Beowulf* in this chapter and throughout the book are from *Beowulf and the Fight at Finnsburg*, ed. F. Klaeber (Boston: Heath, 1950), and will be indicated by line number.

2. E. G. Stanley discusses the connection between meter and diction in "Old English Poetic Diction and the Interpretation of *The Wanderer, The Seafarer* and *The Penitent's Prayer*," *Anglia* 73 (1956): 413–66. Emphasizing the more mechanical aspect of poetic diction he asserts, for example, that some circumlocutions are "not so much the result of figurative thought as of the requirements of the metre; for metre depends on nouns rather than verbs for stress" (428).

3. Creed answers this question by adjusting his critical approach to fit the specific demands of the poem, by searching for the "*kinds* of excellence . . . possible in an art built on formulas" (98).

4. There are some exceptions, notably John Miles Foley who uses reader-response or "receptionalist" theory in his studies of heroic epic and oral tradition. See, for example, "Tradition and the Collective Talent: Oral Epic, Textual Meaning, and Receptionalist Theory," *Cultural Anthropology* vol 1, no. 2 (1986): 203–22. See also John D. Niles, "The Listening Audience," in *Beowulf: The Poem and Its Tradition* (Cambridge: Harvard University Press, 1983), 205–12, and Alain Renoir, "Oral-Formulaic Rhetoric: An Approach to Image and Message in Medieval Poetry," *Medieval Texts and Contemporary Readers*, ed. Laurie A. Finke and Martin B. Schichtman (Ithaca: Cornell University Press, 1987), 234–53. Renoir adopts an anthropological approach to audience reception of oral-formulaic poetry, but also implies a "modicum of agreement" (241) with a basic premise of reader-response criticism—that is, that the reader/hearer is implicated in the construction of meaning.

5. For a variety of analyses of the act of reading and for a comprehensive overview of this field, see *Reader-Response Criticism*, ed. Jane P. Tompkins (Bal-

timore: Johns Hopkins University Press, 1980). In addition to the essays, Tompkins includes an extensive annotated bibliography divided into theoretical and applied approaches. See also *The Reader in the Text*, ed. Susan R. Suleiman and Inge Crosman (Princeton University Press, 1980).

6. See, for example, Hans Robert Jauss, *Toward an Aesthetic of Reception*, tr. Timothy Bahti (Minneapolis: University of Minnesota Press, 1982); Jauss's viewpoint is that literary history should be rewritten as a history of reader's reactions: "In the triangle of author, work and public the last is no passive part, no chain of mere reactions, but rather itself an energy formative of history. The historical life of a literary work is unthinkable without the active participation of its addressees" (19). Edward W. Said discusses the larger cultural implications of texts as events in *The World, the Text, and the Critic* (Cambridge: Harvard University Press, 1983): "My position is that texts are worldly, to some degree they are events, and, even when they appear to deny it, they are nevertheless a part of the social world, human life, and of course the historical moments in which they are located and interpreted" (4).

7. The literature on metaphor and metonymy is too prolific to list here comprehensively. The following are some examples of the variety and scope of the critical applications of the two modes. Jacques Lacan, "Agency of the Letter in the Unconscious" in *Ecrits*, tr. Alan Sheridan (New York: Norton, 1977), 146–78, discusses metonymy and metaphor in terms of desire; Jane Gallop's chapter "Metaphor and Metonymy" in *Reading Lacan* (Ithaca: Cornell University Press, 1985) offers a feminist gloss on Lacan's interpretation; Alice Jardine analyzes the role of the two modes in *Gynesis* (Ithaca: Cornell University Press, 1985), in a feminist critique of the breakdown of narrative, 68–87. For an excellent synthesis of linguistic, psychoanalytic, and semiotic constructions of metaphor and metonymy, see Kaja Silverman, *The Subject of Semiotics* (New York and Oxford: Oxford University Press, 1983), 87–125. Susan Handelman discusses the parallels between metaphor and metonymy, and patristic and rabbinical modes of interpretation, throughout *The Slayers of Moses* (Albany: SUNY Press, 1982). Naomi Schor, *Reading in Detail* (London: Methuen, 1987), considers the esthetic implications of the two figures as they are discovered in the history of art.

8. My suggestion of the coexistence of a variety of embedded cultural meanings within one text will no doubt recall the Bakhtinian thesis of dialogization, although I have not used his specific terminology. In *The Dialogic Imagination*, tr. Caryl Emerson and Michael Holquist (Austin: University of Texas Press, 1981), dialogism is the condition of continual interaction of meanings in a text/world governed by heteroglossia; the dialogic imperative precludes the possibility of monologue, or a single, unitary, authorized reading.

9. There are many examples of this kind of complex semantic layering, of words and epithets from the pagan heroic tradition carrying over into Christian poetry. In many instances the modern editor's capitalization must serve to indicate the difference between the earthly lord (*hlaford, dryhten*) and his eternal counterpart (*Hlaford, Dryhten*), while in *The Dream of the Rood*, for example, Christ and his disciples are described in heroic warrior epithets for lord and retainers.

10. For a discussion of the "metaphysics of presence," see Derrida's essay "Différance" in *Speech and Phenomena*, tr. David B. Allison (Evanston: Northwestern University Press, 1973).

11. We need not rely solely on modern critical apparatus to explain the experience of this poetry. Losing self in a text, taking on or becoming the text, allowing the text to become a vehicle for the construction of meaning and identity are all more complex transactions if one presupposes a modern "self" to be lost; but it should be remembered that all these transactions are associated with the audience-participatory extremes of oral tradition. Shippey (*Old English Verse* [London: Hutchinson University Library, 1972]) reminds those "for whom ancient epic has

been a matter of silence, dictionaries and the printed text" that the "one common element in the descriptions of barbarian narrative is the violence of audience response" (10).

Although we may hesitate to identify with the indignity of abandon, described by Sidonius and recounted by Shippey, of the "gluttonous Burgundian who smears his hair with rancid butter" (11), we can recognize and perhaps make some connection with this extreme of being "spoken" by this poetry. Niles also encourages the modern reader of *Beowulf* to try to connect with the participatory element that was far more pronounced for the poem's original audience: "When readers pick up *Beowulf* privately today and study it as it was never studied in Anglo-Saxon times, they can perhaps gain some additional insight into it by putting themselves in the place of original listeners, who did not have the text before them but entered an arena in which speaker and audience participated in a game of the imagination" (*Beowulf: The Poem and Its Tradition* [Cambridge: Harvard University Press, 1983], 206).

12. Lacan calls attention to the primacy of metonymy and its connection to the "real"; metonymy is a figure that installs "lack-in-being" and configures desire as lack, an absence that apparently compares favorably with the illusion of presence implied by metaphor: "the truth can be evoked only in that dimension of alibi in which all 'realism' in creative works takes its virtue from metonymy" ("Agency of the Letter in the Unconscious," in *Ecrits*, tr. Alan Sheridan [New York: Norton, 1977], 166).

13. For an extended discussion of this overlapping or fusion of literality and figurality in *Genesis B*, see Jane Chance's remarks on Eve in *Woman as Hero in Old English Literature* (Syracuse: Syracuse University Press, 1986), 65–79.

14. For arguments for the formulaic and conventional aspects of this passage, see George Clark. "The Traveller Recognizes His Goal: A Theme in Anglo-Saxon Poetry," *JEGP* 62 (1965): 645–59; Theodore Anderson, *Early Epic Scenery* (Ithaca: Cornell University Press, 1976), 146–52; and Lee C. Ramsey, "The Sea-Voyages in *Beowulf*," *NM* 72 (1971): 51–59. For a discussion of the liveliness and individual artistry of this passage despite its traditional context, see Stanley B. Greenfield, "*Beowulf* 207b–228: Narrative and Descriptive Art," *N & Q* 211 (1966): 86–90. For a different view of the literal and realistic geographical possibilities of the same passage, see my essay "Reinventing Beowulf's Voyage to Denmark," *OEN* vol. 21, no. 2 (Spring 1988): 30–39.

15. Alain Renoir uses the film analogy in "Point of View and Design for Terror in *Beowulf*," *Neuphilologische Mitteilungen* 63 (1962): 154–67. See also N. D. Isaacs, *Structural Principles in Old English Poetry* (Knoxville: University of Tennessee Press, 1968). References to film-making techniques occur throughout the book, but are concentrated in chapter 9, "The One-Man Band of *Christ and Satan*," 127–44. Recent film criticism also makes use of the concept of metonymy; see, for example, Teresa de Lauretis, *Alice Doesn't: Feminism, Semiotics, Cinema* (Bloomington: Indiana University Press, 1984).

16. References to *The Wanderer* are from *The Exeter Book* (ASPR vol. 3), ed. G. P. Krapp and E. V. K. Dobbie (New York: Columbia University Press, 1936).

17. The translations from this point on are my own, except where otherwise indicated. In this chapter I have retained the half-line spacing because it helps visually explicate some of the points I am making about metonymic structure. In the following chapters, I have normalized the translations in the interests of readability and have put them into modern English sentence form. In all my translations, I aim for simplicity and literality rather than elegance.

18. References to *Christ and Satan* are from *The Junius Manuscript* (ASPR vol. 1), ed. G. P. Krapp (New York: Columbia University Press, 1931).

19. For an extended discussion of the many possibilities of sound-sense interaction, see Stanley B. Greenfield, "The Play of Sound and Sense," 84–108, in

The Interpretation of Old English Poems (London: Routledge & Kegan Paul, 1972).

20. References to *Daniel* are from *The Junius Manuscript* (ASPR vol. 1), ed. G. P. Krapp (New York: Columbia University Press, 1931).

21. I argue this point in greater detail in "Nebuchadnezzar's Conversion in the Old English *Daniel*: A Psychological Portrait," *Papers on Language and Literature*, vol. 20, no. 1 (1984): 3–14.

Chapter 2. Swords and Signs

1. Frantzen gives several examples of editors' emendations changing or creating meaning in the poem in "Writing the Unreadable *Beowulf*: 'Writan' and 'Forwritan', the Pen and the Sword," in *Desire for Origins: Anglo-Saxon Studies in Postmodern America* (forthcoming from Rutgers University Press, 1990). He cites a typical emendation occurring at line 6, where *eorl* is usually emended to *eorlas*; perhaps, Frantzen suggests, because "just one opponent for Scyld Scefing is not enough." See also Frantzen and Venegoni, "The Desire for Origins: An Archaeology of Anglo-Saxon Studies," *Style* vol. 20, no. 2 (1986): 142–56, for an overview of the ideological assumptions that have shaped the course and nature of scholarship in both poetry and prose.

2. Studies of art and poetry in the Anglo-Saxon period include: John Leyerle, "The Interlace Structure of *Beowulf*," *University of Toronto Quarterly* vol. 37 (1967–68): 1–17; Lewis E. Nicholson, "The Art of Interlace in *Beowulf*," *Studia Neophilologica* 52 (1980): 237–50; Peter R. Schroeder, "Stylistic Analogies between Old English Art and Poetry," *Viator* 5 (1974): 185–97; Jackson J. Campbell, "Some Aspects of Meaning in Anglo-Saxon Art and Literature," *Annuale Mediaevale* 15 (1974): 5–45; and Richard A. Lewis, "Old English Poetry: Alliteration and Structural Interlace," *Language and Style* 6 (1973): 196–205. John D. Niles discusses the cumulative and cyclical aspects of *Beowulf* in "Ring Composition and the Structure of *Beowulf*," *PMLA* 94 (1979): 924–35; he sees his study as a continuation of Leyerle's work on interlace (933n). See also the "Style and Structure" section of Niles's *Beowulf: The Poem and its Tradition* (Cambridge: Harvard University Press, 1983). For an extended discussion of artistic and literary structural principles in several Old English poems, see Bernard F. Huppé, *The Web of Words* (Albany: SUNY Press), 1970. Ruth Mellinkoff looks at some connections between serpentine imagery in manuscript illumination and biblical texts in "Serpent Imagery in the Illustrated Old English Hexateuch," *Modes of Interpretation in Old English Literature*, ed. Phyllis Rugg Brown, Georgia Ronan Crampton, and Fred C. Robinson (Toronto: University of Toronto Press, 1986), 51–64.

3. For an overview, see Jonathan Evans, "Medieval Studies and Semiotics: Perspectives on Research," *Semiotics 1984*, ed. John Deely (New York: University Press of America, 1985), 511–21. The 1986 volume of *Style* is devoted to a variety of articles on medieval semiotics; see especially Martin Irvine, "Anglo-Saxon Literary Theory Exemplified in Old English Poems: Interpreting the Cross in *The Dream of the Rood* and *Elene*," 157–81, and Evans, "Episodes in Analysis of Medieval Narrative," in *Style* vol. 20, no. 2 (1986): 126–41. For specific reference to *Beowulf*, see Evans's "Irony and Ambiguity in the Medieval Dragon Code," *Semiotics 1982*, ed. John Deely and Jonathan Evans (New York: University Press of America, 1983), 141–50. Evans is editing a forthcoming collection of essays entitled *Semiotica Mediaevalia*. All volumes of *Semiotics* since 1984 contain a separate section on medieval narrative and sign theory, and the 1987 volume of *Semiotica* is a special medieval studies issue. See also Eugene Vance, *Mervelous Signals: Poetics and Sign Theory in the Middle Ages* (Lincoln: University of Nebraska Press, 1986); Paul Zumthor, *Speaking of the Middle Ages*, tr. Sarah White (Lincoln: University of Nebraska Press, 1986).

4. See, for example, John Mahoney's dissertation, "The Monodramatic Structure of *Beowulf*" (Auburn, 1975), which applies Peircean models to the poem.

5. References to Peirce's work are from several sources: *The Collected Papers of Charles Sanders Peirce*, 8 vols., ed. C. Hartshorne and P. Weiss (vols. 1–6), and A. Burks (vols. 7–8) (Cambridge: Harvard University Press, 1931–58; reprinted 1965–66, 8 vols. in 4). References to the *Collected Papers* will follow the standard notation of volume and paragraph number, e.g., 5.591. References to Peirce's *The New Elements of Mathematics*, 4 vols., ed. Carolyn Eisele (The Hague: Mouton, 1976) will be prefaced by NE, e.g., NE1.343. References to *Semiotics and Significs: The Correspondence Between Charles Peirce and Victoria Lady Welby*, ed. Charles S. Hardwick (Bloomington: Indiana University Press, 1977) will be to the editor, e.g., Hardwick, 31.

6. See Silverman's section on Peirce in *The Subject of Semiotics* (New York and Oxford: Oxford University Press, 1983), 14–25, and de Lauretis, chapter 6 of *Alice Doesn't: Feminism, Semiotics, Cinema* (Bloomington: Indiana University Press, 1984), "Semiotics and Experience," especially 172–81. For a discussion of Peirce's concept of subjectivity and its implications for literary criticism, see Walter Benn Michaels, "The Interpreter's Self: Peirce on the Cartesian 'Subject,'" *Reader-Response Criticism*, ed. Jane P. Tompkins (Baltimore: Johns Hopkins University Press, 1980), 185–200.

7. For one of the best introductions to Peirce, which gives a particularly lucid overview and an explanation and breakdown of Peirce's categories and terminology, see chapter 1, "Peirce's Semeiotic," in Michael Shapiro's *The Sense of Grammar: Language as Semeiotic* (Bloomington: Indiana University Press, 1983), 25–72. Another useful introduction is Max H. Fisch, "Peirce's General Theory of Signs," in *Sight, Sound, and Sense*, ed. Thomas A. Sebeok (Bloomington: Indiana University Press, 1978), 31–70. Silverman and de Lauretis (quoted above) discuss Peirce's connections to contemporary semiotic theory and the applications of his sign theory. See also John K. Sherriff, "Charles S. Peirce and the Semiotics of Literature," in *Semiotic Themes*, ed. Richard T. de George (Lawrence: University of Kansas Publications, 1981), 51–74.

8. Peirce's further definitions of the phenomenological categories include the following: "Firstness is the mode of being of that which is such as it is, positively and without reference to anything else. Secondness is the mode of being of that which is such as it is, with respect to a second but regardless of any third. Thirdness is the mode of being of that which is such as it is, in bringing a second and third into relation to each other" (Hardwick, 24).

9. "An *Icon* is a sign which refers to the Object that it denotes merely by virtue of characters of its own, and which it possesses, just the same, whether any such Object exists or not" (2.243).

"The icon has no dynamical connection with the object it represents; it simply happens that its qualities resemble those of that object" (2.299).

"A pure icon can convey no positive or factual information. . . . But it is of the utmost value for enabling its interpreter to study what would be the character of such an object in case any such did exist. Geometry sufficiently illustrates that" (4.447).

"Of a completely opposite nature is the kind of representamen (sign) termed an *index*. This is a real thing or fact which is a sign of its object by virtue of being connected with it as a matter of fact and also by forcibly intruding upon the mind, quite regardless of its being interpreted as a sign" (4.447).

"Indices . . . direct the attention to their objects by blind compulsion" (2.306).

"Because compulsion is essentially *hic et nunc,* the occasion of the compulsion can only be represented to the listener by compelling him to have experience of that same occasion. Hence it is requisite that there should be a sign which shall act dynamically upon the reader's attention. . . . Such a sign I call an *Index*" (2.336).

". . . It [the index] is in dynamical (including spatial] connection both with the individual object, on the one hand, and with the senses or memory of the person for whom it serves as a sign, on the other hand." (2.305).

"A Symbol is a representamen [sign] whose representative character consists precisely in its being a rule that will determine its Interpretant" (2.292).

"A Symbol is a law, or regularity of the indefinite future" (2.293).

"The being of a symbol consists in the real fact that something surely will be experienced if certain conditions be satisfied. Namely, it will influence the thought and conduct of its interpreter" (4.447).

10. See Dodwell's chapter, "Anglo-Saxon Taste," in *Anglo-Saxon Art: A New Perspective* (Ithaca: Cornell University Press, 1982), 24–43, where he repeatedly refers to and demonstrates this "love of resplendence." In this chapter, and throughout the book, Dodwell provides an impressive, extensive collection of examples of the variety of objects customarily adorned with gold or silver.

11. In an argument that affirms the positive connotations of treasure, Niles dismisses the notion that Beowulf displayed greed for treasure at the end of the poem. Such a supposition "starts from the premise that all treasure is evil, a point of view that was not common in England and that the poet did not share" (1983: 220); the treasure buried with the hero is simply "*lof* made visible" (222).

12. See Cherniss, chapter 4, "Treasure: The Material Symbol of Human Worth," in *Ingeld and Christ: Heroic Concepts and Christian Values in Old English Christian Poetry* (The Hague: Mouton, 1972).

13. See R. L. S. Bruce-Mitford, *The Sutton Hoo Ship Burial* (London: The Trustees of the British Museum, 1968), 19 and 34–35, for a discussion of the missing body in the Sutton Hoo burial.

14. For a detailed discussion of these and other descriptive epithets for swords, see Caroline Brady's comprehensive study, " 'Weapons' in *Beowulf*: An Analysis of the Nominal Compounds and an Evaluation of the Poet's Use of Them," *Anglo-Saxon England* 8 (1979): 79–141. See also A. T. Hatto, "Snake-swords and Boar-helms in *Beowulf,*" *ES* 38 (1957): 145–60.

15. See lines 2584–85 and 2680–82 in *Beowulf*. Taylor Culbert discusses these passages in detail in "The Narrative Function of Beowulf's Swords," *JEGP* 59 (Jan. 1960): 13–20.

16. 1521–22. See also Robinson's comments on this passage and personification in *Beowulf* in *Beowulf and the Appositive Style* (Knoxville: University of Tennessee Press, 1985), 73.

17. It should be noted that the interchangeability of words, deeds, and things forms a system of circulation, a chain of signification, in which the women of the poem do not participate. For a discussion of the nature and implications of this exclusion, see chapter 3, 85ff.

18. The concept of "inscription in the flesh," a notion that Deleuze and Guattari develop from Nietzsche, is examined in more detail in chapter 3, 89–90.

19. This kind of analysis has been attempted before, especially in the art/poetry discussions cited in note 2, where themes, motifs, and recurrent patterns are examined. As far as I am aware, there has been no attempt to analyze sign interaction in specifically Peircean terms. I have come across one dissertation, "The Monodramatic Structure of *Beowulf,*" by John Mahoney (Auburn, 1975),

which applies the icon/index/symbol trichotomy to larger structural patterns and rhetorical modes but not to the individual signs in the poem.

20. See chapter 3, 81, for a further discussion of the relation, structural and thematic, between these two women.

21. R. E. Kaske, in "Weohstan's Sword," *MLN* 75 (1960): 465–68, and Adrien Bonjour, in "Weohstan's Slaying of Eanmund," *ES* 27 (1946): 14–19, present two divergent points of view about the primary significance of this "digression." Kaske sees it as a way to illustrate the ideal of good retainership, whereas Bonjour sees it as a way of connecting all the events associated with the sword. A Peircean model of sign interaction, however, can accommodate both points of view; it can encompass the variety of the sword signs' connotations and account for their dynamic interaction.

22. For a longer discussion of Peirce, teleology, and artistic semeiosis, see Michael Shapiro, "Remarks on the Nature of the Autotelic Sign," *Georgetown University Roundtable on Languages and Linguistics 1982* (Washington, D.C.: Georgetown University Press, 1982), 101–11.

23. See chapter 1, 11.

24. As the poem is poised between Secondness and Thirdness, it is also poised between correlated types of interpretants, dynamic and final. I have referred only to Peirce's second trichotomy of interpretants, immediate/dynamic/final; this overlaps with the first trichotomy, emotional/energetic/logical, to produce some much finer cross-distinctions, which might also describe this "fence" or place between experience and language that the poem can inhabit. Peirce's categories minutely and repeatedly intersect, making for subtleties of definition that I have not been able to address in this short study. One can have a dynamic logical interpretant, or "Firstnesses of Firstness, of Secondness and of Thirdness" (Shapiro, 1983: 53). For further discussion of these distinctions, I again refer the reader to Michael Shapiro's chapter on Peirce's semeiotic, and to T. L. Short's essay, "Semeiosis and Intentionality," *Transactions of the Charles S. Peirce Society* 17 (1981): 197–223.

Chapter 3. Gender and Interpretation

1. See Jane Gallops's extended discussion of the two tropes and their connections to masculine and feminine desire in chapter 5, "Metaphor and Metonymy," *Reading Lacan* (Ithaca: Cornell University Press, 1985). Luce Irigaray distinguishes metaphoric "solidity" from metonymic "fluidity" and examines both constructs in terms of psychoanalytic neglect of femininity and privileging of masculinity in "The 'Mechanics of Fluids,'" *This Sex Which Is Not One*, tr. Catherine Porter (Ithaca: Cornell University Press, 1985). See also Jacqueline Rose's, Introduction to *Feminine Sexuality. Jacques Lacan and the Ecole Freudienne*, ed. Juliet Mitchell and Jacqueline Rose (London: Macmillan, 1982), where the terms of connection of sexuality and language recall metaphoricity ("fixing of meaning") and metonymy ("verbal slippage").

2. "Economy" is used as a comprehensive term for the complex of cultural systems of change and exchange, wherein power is sought, claimed, and distributed; "masculine economy" denotes the social and material conditions of patriarchy, in which women may be construed as commodities in the system of change and exchange of power relations between men.

3. See, for example, the analysis of narrative technique in the Finnsburg episode in Thomas Shippey, *Old English Verse* (London: Hutchinson, 1971), 19–30. Shippey emphasizes the ambiguity and problematic aspects of heroic choice, and shows how the poet is concerned with mental and emotional acts rather than physical ones, concentrating on the "inner maelstrom" (24) experienced by the characters.

4. "Symbolic," capitalized, represents Lacan's specific use of the term. Betsy Wing, translator of Cixous and Clément's *The Newly Born Woman* (Minneapolis: University of Minnesota Press, 1986), glosses the term (see pages 163–68); although there can be no pure instance of the Symbolic, Lacan sees language as the primary vehicle for the abstract order of discursive and symbolic action. Elsewhere I have followed Cixous and Clement's more general, uncapitalized use of the term; the symbolic order is the complex of symbolic systems that comprises and expresses a culture.

5. From *Moses and Monotheism*, quoted by Cixous and Clément in their discussion of "The Dawn of Phallocentrism" (100).

6. References to the nonexistence/nonidentity of woman are found throughout Lacan's *Télèvision* (Editions du Seuil, 1973). See also Jane Gallop, *The Daughter's Seduction: Feminism and Psychoanalysis* (Ithaca: Cornell University Press, 1982) for a discussion of Lacan's views on women, especially chapter 3 "The Ladies' Man," 33–42.

7. Earl parallels the decline in the legal rights of women in the Anglo-Saxon period to the diminishment of the power and influence of the kinship system; this process, he suggests, supports "Freud's view of woman's role as the antagonist of civilization: 'Women represent the interests of the family and of sexual life. The work of civilization has become increasingly the business of men, it confronts them with ever more difficult tasks and compels them to carry out instinctual sublimations of which women are little capable. . . . Thus the woman finds herself forced into the background by the claims of civilization and she adopts a hostile attitude towards it'" (1983: 146).

8. I have selected Renoir's comments in "A Reading Context for *The Wife's Lament*" to characterize one view of the passivity of women in Old English poetry; I should add that Renoir has argued elsewhere for the assertive logic and intelligence of Eve in "Eve's IQ Rating: Two Sexist Views of *Genesis B*," paper delivered at MLA Convention, Houston, 1980.

9. For a good selection of examples of Anglo-Saxon women in public, religious, and political life, see Joan Nicholson's "*Feminae Gloriosae*: Women in the Age of Bede," 15–29, and Pauline Stafford's "Sons and Mothers: Family Politics in the Early Middle Ages," 79–100, both in *Medieval Women*, ed. Derek Baker (Oxford: Basil Blackwell, 1978).

10. See Sheila C. Dietrich, "An Introduction to Women in Anglo-Saxon Society (c. 600–1066)," in *The Women of England*, ed. Barbara Kanner (Hamden, Conn.: Archon Books, 1979), 32–56. Dietrich sees a decline in the status of women within the church later in the period (38); her essay also provides a thorough survey of differing views on women throughout the period. Christine Fell, in *Women in Anglo-Saxon England* (Oxford: Basil Blackwell, 1986), discusses the issue of the critical division of views concerning the relationship of Christianity and women in her Introduction, and also offers another view of both male and female status: "the equality of the sexes, which flourished in the eighth century in learning and in literacy, was replaced in the tenth century by equality in ignorance" (128).

11. For example, Barrie Ruth Strauss, "Women's Words as Weapons: Speech as Action in 'The Wife's Lament,'" *Texas Studies in Literature and Language* vol. 23 (Summer 1981): 268–85; Bernice W. Kliman, "Women in Early English Literature, *Beowulf* to the *Ancrene Wisse*," *Nottingham Medieval Studies* 21 (1977): 32–49. For a breakdown of recent scholarship, see Alexandra Hennessey Olsen, "Women in *Beowulf*," in *Approaches to Teaching Beowulf*, ed. Jess B. Bessinger, Jr., and Robert F. Yeager (New York: Modern Language Association of America, 1984), 150–56. Two recent conference papers approach the subject of women in Old English poetry from nonbinary theoretical perspectives: Joan Blythe, "Caves of Desire and Verbal Slippage in *The Wife's Lament*," and Helen Bennett, "In a Different Voice: Feminism,

Post-Structuralism, and Two Old English Elegies," both presented at the 22nd International Congress on Medieval Studies, Kalamazoo, 1987.

12. Damico does not find this a significant drawback, arguing for the *Beowulf* poet's thorough knowledge of matters Scandinavian and the continuity and consistency of Scandinavian poetic tradition. See her Preface, x–xi.

13. See Chapter 3, note 3, above.

14. Thorstein Veblen introduced the concept of "trained incapacity" in *Theory of the Leisure Class* (London: Macmillan, 1899), applying it primarily to businessmen whose very abilities and training worked against them, functioning in some cases as blindnesses and inadequacies. More recently sociolinguists Shirley and Edwin Ardener have applied the concept to the language of women as part of the "muted group" theory. As members of a "muted group," women must learn to speak the language of the dominant group, a language that is essentially an alien structure not of their own making. This situation makes for many kinds of distortion and incongruity: "For example, the dominant group may provide a style for them such that, if they are perceived as 'birds', when angry they may be required to 'roar like doves'" (Ardener, 20), "The Nature of Women in Society," in *Perceiving Females*, ed. Shirley Ardener (New York: Halsted Press, 1978), 9–49. For an extended discussion of the sociological "muted group" theory and its relation to female language use, see Cheris Kramerae, *Women and Men Speaking* (Rowley, Mass.: Newbury House Publishers, 1981).

15. This point was emphasized by Helen T. Bennett in a discussion of her paper "Revising the Germanic Tradition of Lament to Interpret the Female Mourner at Beowulf's Funeral" (presented at 23rd International Congress on Medieval Studies, Kalamazoo, 1988), where she affirms the female capacity to endure and survive in the poem, to persistently choose life over death.

16. See chapter 2, above.

17. See especially chapter 2, "Wealhtheow and the Heroic Tradition," 17–40. For a discussion of Wealhtheow's name, see pp. 62–68.

18. The only full-length study of Beowulf's speeches from the point of view of speech act theory that I have come across is Charles E. McNally's dissertation, "'Beowulf Maþelode . . .': Text Linguistics and Speech Acts," SUNY Binghamton, 1975. Elizabeth Closs Traugott makes interesting use of speech act theory in her discussion of Old English in *A History of English Syntax* (New York: Holt, Rinehart and Winston, 1972).

19. Austin and Searle divide the utterance, or speech act, into three stages or levels: the locutionary level, which is the content of the utterance itself; the intention of the speaker, the force or direction of the utterance, which is the illocutionary act (Searle calls this "illocutionary point"); and the perlocutionary act, which is the actual effect, intended or otherwise, of the utterance. Searle's method of classifying illocutionary acts is particularly useful for my purposes because he expands the criteria for examining the illocutionary act, and makes its complexity and ambiguity more accessible to analysis.

20. Searle defines directives as "attempts (of varying degrees, and hence, more precisely, they are determinates of the determinable which includes attempting) by the speaker to get the hearer to do something. They may be very modest 'attempts' as when I invite you to do it or suggest that you do it, or they may be very fierce attempts as when I insist that you do it. Using the shriek mark for the illocutionary point indicating device for the members of this class generally, we have the following symbolism: ! ↑ W (H does A). The direction of fit (indicated by the arrow) is world-to-words and the sincerity condition is want (or wish or desire). The propositional content is always that the hearer H does some future action A. Verbs denoting members of this class are ask, order, command, request, beg, plead, pray, entreat, and also invite, permit, and advise" (11).

21. See also Damico's note on 185 in support of this interpretation.
22. See Damico, 123–32, for an extended discussion of Wealhtheow's speeches.
23. See Klaeber, 195–99, for a discussion of this passage and an assessment of manuscript emendations. For an extended discussion of her problematic name, see also R. W. Chambers, *Beowulf: An Introduction*, with supplement by C. L. Wrenn (Cambridge: Cambridge University Press, 1963): 36–40, 238–43, 41–42.
24. This is Norman Eliason's argument in "The 'Thryth-Offa Digression' in *Beowulf*," in *Franciplegius: Medieval and Linguistic Studies in Honor of Francis Peabody Magoun, Jr.*, ed. Jess B. Bessinger and Robert P. Creed (New York: New York University Press, 1965), 124–38; Eliason maintains that the entire "digression" refers to Hygd.
25. Kemp Malone, "*Beowulf*," reprinted in *An Anthology of Beowulf Criticism*, ed. Lewis E. Nicholson (Notre Dame: University of Notre Dame Press, 1963), 148–49. See also Adrian Bonjour, *The Digressions in Beowulf* (Medium Aevum Monographs 5, Oxford: Basil Blackwell, 1950), 53–55.
26. Extending and often transforming the work of Freud and Lacan, recent feminist critics have focused on the masculine tyranny of the gaze and the notion of woman as a mirror for male subjectivity as a fertile source for new theoretical metaphors and feminist insights. See chapter 7, "Patriarchal Reflections: Luce Irigaray's Looking-glass," in Toril Moi, *Sexual/Textual Politics* (London: Methuen, 1985), 127–49. Moi pays specific attention to Irigaray's punning examination of female "specul(ariz)ation" and mimicry.
27. Chance suggests that the structural location of the passage "invites a comparison of this stubborn princess and the two other 'queens,' Hygd and the *wif* (Grendel's mother)" (105). She also points out that Modthryth and Grendel's mother are connected by the same irony: as Modthryth weaves "deadly bonds" for her suitors, thereby severing the bonds of peace, "she resembles that other ironic peace-weaver, the *wif*, who tried to penetrate the braided breast-net of Beowulf with her knife" (106). Damico sees them as parts of a valkyrie-inspired whole: "Because they are parallel in function and nature, collectively Modthrytho and Grendel's mother may form one half of a valkyrie-diptych configuration" (51).
28. Although Modthryth's violence might seem anomalous in the human, female context of the poem, the Anglo-Saxon period offers plentiful examples of women who were less than temperate. Among others, Pauline Stafford (cited chapter 3, note 9, above) recounts the story of Aelfthryth, mother of Aethelraed Unraed, who helped murder the son of her husband Edgar's first wife in order to secure the succession for her own son (79–80), and records the career of Eadburh, who murdered her husband's followers and finally her husband himself in her attempts to secure power (83). Coincidentally, Eadburh was the daughter of Offa of Mercia, supposedly the descendant of Offa of the Angles, Modthryth's husband.

Bibliography

Anderson, Theodore. *Early Epic Scenery*. Ithaca: Cornell University Press, 1976.

Ardener, Shirley. "The Nature of Women in Society," *Perceiving Females*. Ed. Shirley Ardener. New York: Halsted Press, 1978, 9–49.

Austin, J. L. *How To Do Things With Words*. New York: Oxford University Press, 1962.

Bakhtin, M. M. *The Dialogic Imagination*. Tr. Caryl Emerson and Michael Holquist. Austin: University of Texas Press, 1981.

Barthes, Roland. *Image-Music-Text*. Tr. Stephen Heath. New York: Hill & Wang, 1977.

Binns, A. L. "'Linguistic' Reading: Two Suggestions of the Quality of Literature," *Essays on Style and Language: Linguistic and Critical Approaches to Literary Style*. Ed. Roger Fowler. New York: Humanities Press, 1966, 118–34.

Bloomfield, Morton W. "'Interlace' as a Medieval Narrative Technique with Special Reference to *Beowulf*," *Magister Regis: Studies in Honor of R. E. Kaske*. Ed. Arthur Groos. New York: Fordham University Press, 1986, 49–59.

Bonjour, Adrien. "Weohstan's Slaying of Eanmund," *English Studies* 27 (1946): 14–19.

———. *The Digressions in Beowulf*. Medium Aevum Monographs V. Oxford: Basil Blackwell, 1950.

Brady, Caroline. "'Weapons' in *Beowulf*: An Analysis of the Nominal Compounds and an Evaluation of the Poet's Use of Them," *Anglo-Saxon England* 8 (1979): 79–141.

Bruce-Mitford, R. L. S. *The Sutton Hoo Ship Burial*. London: The Trustees of the British Museum, 1968.

Campbell, Jackson, J. "Some Aspects of Meaning in Anglo-Saxon Art and Literature," *Annuale Mediaevale* 15 (1974): 5–45.

Chambers, R. W. *Beowulf: An Introduction*. With supplement by C. L. Wrenn. Cambridge: Cambridge University Press, 1963.

Chance, Jane. *Woman as Hero in Old English Poetry*. Syracuse: Syracuse University Press, 1986.

Cherniss, M. D. *Ingeld and Christ: Heroic Concepts and Christian Values in Old English Poetry*. The Hague: Mouton, 1972.

————. "The Cross as Christ's Weapon: The Influence of Heroic Literary Tradition on *The Dream of the Rood*," *Anglo-Saxon England* 2 (1973): 241–52.

Cixous, Hélène, and Catherine Clément. *The Newly Born Woman*. Tr. Betsy Wing. Minneapolis: University of Minnesota Press, 1986.

Clark, George. "The Traveller Recognizes His Goal: A Theme in Anglo-Saxon Poetry," *JEGP* 62 (1965): 645–59.

Cramer, Carmen. "The Voice of Beowulf," *Germanic Notes* 8 (1977): 40–44.

Creed, Robert P. "On the Possibility of Criticizing Old English Poetry," *Texas Studies in Literature and Language* 3 (1961): 97–106.

Crossley-Holland, Kevin. *Beowulf*. New York: Farrar, Strauss and Giroux, 1968.

Culbert, Taylor. "The Narrative Function of Beowulf's Swords," *JEGP* 59 (January 1960): 13–20.

Damico, Helen. *Beowulf's Wealhtheow and the Valkyrie Tradition*. Madison: University of Wisconsin Press, 1984.

Davidson, H. E. *The Sword in Anglo-Saxon England*. Oxford: Clarendon Press, 1962.

De Lauretis, Teresa. *Alice Doesn't: Feminism, Semiotics, Cinema*. Bloomington: Indiana University Press, 1984.

————. *Technologies of Gender*. Bloomington: Indiana University Press, 1987.

Deleuze, Gilles, and Felix Guattari. *Anti-Oedipus*. Tr. Robert Hurley, Mark Seem, and Helen R. Lane. New York: Viking Press, 1977.

Derrida, Jacques. "Structure, Sign, and Play in the Discourse of the Human Sciences," *The Structuralist Controversy*. Ed. Richard Macksey and Eugenio Donato. Baltimore: Johns Hopkins University Press, 1972, 247–72.

————. *Speech and Phenomena*. Tr. David B. Allison. Evanston: Northwestern University Press, 1973.

Dietrich, Sheila. "An Introduction to Women in Anglo-Saxon Society," *The Women of England*. Ed. Barbara Kanner. Hamden, Conn.: Archon Books, 1979, 32–56.

Dodwell, Charles R. *Anglo-Saxon Art: A New Perspective*. Ithaca: Cornell University Press, 1982.

Donaldson, E. Talbot, tr. *Beowulf: A New Prose Translation*. New York: Norton, 1966.

Earl, James W. "The Necessity of Evil in *Beowulf*," *South Atlantic Bulletin* 44 (1979): 81–98.

————. "The Role of the Men's Hall in the Development of the Anglo-Saxon Superego," *Psychiatry* vol. 46 (May 1983): 139–60.

Eco, Umberto. *A Theory of Semiotics*. Bloomington: Indiana University Press, 1976.

Eliason, Norman E. "The 'Thryth-Offa Digression' in *Beowulf*," *Franciplegius: Medieval and Linguistic Studies in Honor of Francis Peabody*

Magoun Jr. Ed. Jess B. Bessinger and Robert P. Creed. New York: New York University Press, 1965, 124–38.

———. "Healfdene's Daughter," *Anglo-Saxon Poetry: Essays in Appreciation.* Eds. Lewis E. Nicholson and Dolores Warwick Frese. Notre Dame: University of Notre Dame Press, 1975, 3–13.

Evans, J. M. "*Genesis B* and Its Background," *Review of English Studies* n.s. 14 (1963): 1–16, 113–23.

Evans, Jonathan. "Irony and Ambiguity in the Medieval Dragon Code," *Semiotics 1982.* Ed. John Deely and Jonathan Evans. New York: University Press of America, 1983, 141–50.

———. "Medieval Studies and Semiotics: Perspectives on Research," *Semiotics 1984.* Ed. John Deely. New York: University Press of America, 1985, 511–21.

———. "Episodes in Analysis of Medieval Narrative," *Style* vol. 20, no. 2 (1986): 126–41.

Fell, Christine. *Women in Anglo-Saxon England.* Oxford: Basil Blackwell, 1986.

Finke, Laurie A., and Martin B. Schichtman, eds. *Medieval Texts and Contemporary Readers.* Ithaca: Cornell University Press, 1987.

Fisch, Max H. "Peirce's General Theory of Signs," *Sight, Sound and Sense.* Ed. Thomas A. Sebeok. Bloomington: Indiana University Press, 1978, 31–70.

Fish, Stanley E. "Literature in the Reader: Affective Stylistics," *Reader-Response Criticism.* Ed. Jane P. Tompkins. Baltimore: Johns Hopkins University Press, 1980, 70–100.

Foley, John Miles. "Tradition and the Collective Talent: Oral Epic, Textual Meaning, and Receptionalist Theory," *Cultural Anthropology* vol 1, no. 2 (1986): 203–22.

Foucault, Michel. "What Is an Author?" *The Foucault Reader.* Ed. Paul Rabinow. New York: Pantheon Books, 1984a, 101–20.

———. "Nietzsche, Genealogy, History." *The Foucault Reader.* Ed. Paul Rabinow. New York: Pantheon Books, 1984b, 76–100.

Frantzen, Allen J. *Desire for Origins: Anglo-Saxon Studies in Postmodern America.* Forthcoming from Rutgers University Press, 1990.

———, and Charles L. Venegoni. "The Desire for Origins: An Archaeological Analysis of Anglo-Saxon Studies," *Style* vol. 20, no. 2 (1986): 142–56.

Freud, Sigmund. "Beyond the Pleasure Principle." *A General Selection from the Works of Sigmund Freud.* Ed. John Rickman. 1920. Garden City, N.Y.: Doubleday, 1957.

———. *New Introductory Lectures on Psychoanalysis.* 1933. Ed. and tr. James Strachey. New York: Norton, 1965.

Gallop, Jane. *The Daughter's Seduction: Feminism and Psychoanalysis.* Ithaca: Cornell University Press, 1982.

———. *Reading Lacan.* Ithaca: Cornell University Press, 1985.

Greenfield, Stanley B. "*Beowulf* 207b–228: Narrative and Descriptive Art," *Notes and Queries* 211 (1966): 86–90.

———. *The Interpretation of Old English Poems.* London and Boston: Routledge and Kegan Paul, 1972.

Handelman, Susan. *The Slayers of Moses.* Albany: State University of New York Press, 1982.

Hans, James S. *Imitation and the Image of Man.* Philadelphia and Amsterdam: John Benjamins Publishing Co., 1987.

Hansen, Elaine Tuttle. "Women in Old English Poetry Reconsidered," *The Michigan Academician* 9 (1976–77): 109–17.

Hardwick, Charles S., ed. *Semiotics and Significs: The Correspondence between Charles Peirce and Victoria Lady Welby.* Bloomington: Indiana University Press, 1977.

Hatto, A. T. "Snake-swords and Boar-helms in *Beowulf,*" *English Studies* 38 (1957): 145–60.

Huppé, Bernard F. *The Web of Words.* Albany: State University of New York Press, 1970.

Irigaray, Luce. *This Sex Which Is Not One.* Tr. Catherine Porter. Ithaca: Cornell University Press, 1985.

Irvine, Martin. "Anglo-Saxon Literary Theory Exemplified in Old English Poems: Interpreting the Cross in *The Dream of the Rood* and *Elene,*" *Style* vol. 20, no. 2 (1986): 157–81.

Irving, E. B. *A Reading of Beowulf.* New Haven: Yale University Press, 1968.

Isaacs, N. D. "The Convention of Personification in *Beowulf,*" *Old English Poetry: Fifteen Essays.* Ed. Robert Creed. Providence: Brown University Press, 1967, 215–48.

Jakobson, Roman. "The Metaphoric and Metonymic Poles," *Selected Writings II.* The Hague: Mouton & Co., 1971, 254–59.

Jardine, Alice. *Gynesis.* Ithaca: Cornell University Press, 1985.

Jauss, Hans Robert. *Toward an Aesthetic of Reception.* Tr. Timothy Bahti. Minneapolis: University of Minnesota Press, 1982.

Kaske, R. E. "Weohstan's Sword," *Modern Language Notes* 75 (1960): 465–68.

Klaeber, F., ed. *Beowulf and the Fight at Finnsburg.* Boston: Heath, 1950.

Kliman, Bernice W. "Women in Early English Literature, *Beowulf* to the *Ancrene Wisse,*" *Nottingham Medieval Studies* 21 (1977): 32–49.

Klinck, Anne. "Female Characterization in Old English Poetry and the Growth of Psychological Realism: *Genesis B* and *Christ I,*" *Neophilologus* 63 (1979): 597–610.

Kramerae, Cheris. *Women and Men Speaking.* Rowley, Mass.: Newbury House Publishers, 1981.

Kristeva, Julia. *About Chinese Women.* Tr. Anita Barrows. New York: Urizen Books, 1977.

———. "The Novel as Polylogue," *Desire in Language: A Semiotic Approach to Literature and Art.* Ed. Leon S. Roudiez. New York: Columbia University Press, 1980, 159–209.

———. "The System and the Speaking Subject," *The Kristeva Reader.* Ed. Toril Moi. New York: Columbia University Press, 1986, 24–33.

Lacan, Jacques. *Télèvision.* Paris: Editions du Seuil. 1973.

———. *Ecrits.* Tr. Alan Sheridan. New York: Norton, 1977.

———. *Four Fundamental Concepts of Psychoanalysis.* Tr. Alan Sheridan. New York: Norton, 1981.

Lewis, Richard A. "Old English Poetry: Alliteration and Structural Interlace," *Language and Style* 6 (1973): 196–205.

Leyerle, John. "The Interlace Structure of *Beowulf,*" *University of Toronto Quarterly* vol. 37 (1967–68): 1–17.

Mahoney, John. "The Monodramatic Structure of *Beowulf.*: DAH 76–02603, August 1975 (Auburn).

Malone, Kemp. "*Beowulf,*" *An Anthology of Beowulf Criticism.* Ed. Lewis Nicholson. Notre Dame: University of Notre Dame Press, 1963, 137–54.

Marino, Matthew. "Linguistics, Literary Criticism and Old English," *Mediaevalia* 5 (1979): 1–14.

McNally, Charles Edward. "'Beowulf Maþelode': Text Linguistics and Speech Acts." DAI 36: 1476A. Sept. 1975 (SUNY Binghamton).

Meese, Elizabeth A. *Crossing the Double-Cross.* Chapel Hill and London: University of North Carolina Press, 1986.

Mellinkoff, Ruth. "Serpent Imagery in the Old English Hexateuch," *Modes of Interpretation in Old English Literature.* Ed. Phyllis Rugg Brown, Georgia Ronan Crampton, and Fred C. Robinson. Toronto: University of Toronto Press, 1986, 51–64.

Michaels, Walter Benn. "The Interpreter's Self: Peirce on the Cartesian 'Subject,'" *Reader-Response Criticism.* Ed. Jane P. Tompkins. Baltimore: Johns Hopkins University Press, 1980, 185–200.

Mitchell, Bruce. "Linguistic Facts and the Interpretation of Old English Poetry," *Anglo-Saxon England* 4 (1975): 11–28.

Mitchell, Juliet, and Jacqueline Rose, eds. *Feminine Sexuality: Jacques Lacan and the Ecole Freudienne.* London: Macmillan, 1982.

Moi, Toril. *Sexual/Textual Politics.* London: Methuen, 1985.

Nicholson, Joan. "*Feminae Gloriosae*: Women in the Age of Bede," *Medieval Women.* Ed. Derek Baker. Oxford: Basil Blackwell, 1978, 15–29.

Nicholson, Lewis E. "Hunlafing and the Point of the Sword," *Anglo-Saxon Poetry: Essays in Appreciation for John C. McGalliard.* Ed. Lewis E. Nicholson and Dolores Warwick Frese. Notre Dame: University of Notre Dame Press, 1975, 50–61.

———. "The Art of Interlace in *Beowulf,*" *Studia Neophilologica* 52 (1980): 237–50.

Nietzsche, Friedrich. *The Birth of Tragedy and The Genealogy of Morals.* Tr.

Francis Golffing. Garden City, N.Y.: Doubleday, 1956.

Niles, John D. "Ring Composition and the Structure of *Beowulf*," *PMLA* 94 (1979): 924–35.

———. *Beowulf: The Poem and Its Tradition.* Cambridge: Harvard University Press, 1983.

Nordenfalk, Carl. *Celtic and Anglo-Saxon Painting.* New York: George Braziller, 1977.

Olsen, Alexandra Hennessey. "Women in *Beowulf*," *Approaches to Teaching Beowulf.* Ed. Jess B. Bessinger, Jr., and Robert F. Yeager. New York: Modern Language Association of America, 1984, 150–56.

Osborn, Marijane. *Beowulf: A Verse Translation with Treasures of the Ancient North.* Berkeley: University of California Press, 1983.

Overing, Gillian R. "Nebuchadnezzar's Conversion in the Old English *Daniel*: A Psychological Portrait," *Papers on Language and Literature* vol. 20, no. 1 (1984): 3–14.

———. "Reinventing Beowulf's Voyage to Denmark," *Old English Newsletter* vol. 21, no. 2 (Spring 1988): 30–39.

Pasternack, Carol Braun. "Stylistic Disjunctions in *The Dream of the Rood*," *Anglo-Saxon England* 13 (1985): 167–86.

Peirce, Charles Sanders. *The Collected Papers of Charles Sanders Peirce.* 8 vols. Ed. C. Hartshorne and P. Weiss (vols. 1–6), and A. Burks (vols. 7–8). Cambridge: Harvard University Press, 1931–58. Reprinted 1965–66, 8 vols. in 4.

———. *The New Elements of Mathematics.* 4 vols. Ed. Carolyn Eisele. The Hague: Mouton, 1976.

Quirk, Randolph. "Poetic Language and Old English Metre," *Essays on the English Language: Medieval and Modern.* Bloomington: Indiana University Press, 1968, 1–19.

Ramsey, Lee C. "The Sea-Voyages in *Beowulf*," *Neuphilologische Mitteilungen* 72 (1971): 51–59.

Renoir, Alain. "Point of View and Design for Terror in *Beowulf*," *Neuphilologische Mitteilungen* 63 (1962): 154–67.

———. "A Reading Context for *The Wife's Lament*." *Anglo-Saxon Poetry: Essays in Appreciation for John C. McGalliard.* Ed. Lewis E. Nicholson and Dolores Warwick Frese. Notre Dame: Notre Dame University Press, 1975, 224–41.

———. "Oral-Formulaic Rhetoric: An Approach to Image and Message in Medieval Poetry," *Medieval Texts and Contemporary Readers.* Ed. Laurie A. Finke and Martin B. Schichtman. Ithaca: Cornell University Press, 1987, 234–53.

Ricoeur, Paul. "Violence and Language," *Political and Social Essays.* Eds. David Stewart, Joseph Bien. Athens: Ohio University Press, 1974, 88–101.

———. "Metaphor and the Main Problem of Hermeneutics," *The Philosophy of Paul Ricoeur.* Ed. Charles E. Reagan and David Stewart. Boston:

Beacon Press, 1978, 134–48.

Robinson, Fred C. "Teaching the Backgrounds: History, Religion, Culture," in *Approaches to Teaching Beowulf.* Ed. Jess B. Bessinger and Robert F. Yeager. Modern Language Association of America: 1984, 107–22.

———. *Beowulf and the Appositive Style.* Knoxville: University of Tennessee Press, 1985.

Said, Edward W. *Beginnings: Intention and Method.* Baltimore: Johns Hopkins University Press, 1975.

———. *The World, the Text, and the Critic.* Cambridge: Harvard University Press, 1983.

Schor, Naomi. *Reading in Detail.* London: Methuen, 1987.

Schroeder, Peter. "Stylistic Analogies Between Old English Art and Poetry," *Viator* 5 (1974): 185–97.

Searle, John R. "A Classification of Illocutionary Acts." *Language in Society* 5 (April 1976): 1–23.

Shapiro, Michael. "Remarks on the Nature of the Autotelic Sign," *Georgetown University Roundtable on Languages and Linguistics 1982.* Washington, D.C.: Georgetown University Press, 1982, 101–11.

———. *The Sense of Grammar: Language as Semeiotic.* Bloomington: Indiana University Press, 1983.

Sherriff, John K. "Charles S. Peirce and the Semiotics of Literature," *Semiotic Themes.* Ed. Richard T. DeGeorge. Lawrence: University of Kansas Publications, 1981, 51–74.

Shippey, Thomas O. *Old English Verse.* London: Hutchinson University Library, 1972.

Short, T. L. "Semeiosis and Intentionality," *Transactions of the Charles S. Peirce Society* 17 (1981): 197–223.

Silverman, Kaja. *The Subject of Semiotics.* New York: Oxford University Press, 1983.

Sklute, Larry M. "*Freoðuwebbe* in Old English Poetry." *Neuphilologische Mitteilungen* 71 (1970): 534–41.

Stafford, Pauline. "Sons and Mothers: Family Politics in the Early Middle Ages," *Medieval Women.* Ed. Derek Baker. Oxford: Basil Blackwell, 1978, 79–100.

Stanley, E. G. "Old English Poetic Diction and the Interpretation of *The Wanderer, The Seafarer* and *The Penitent's Prayer,*" *Anglia* 73 (1956): 413–66.

Steiner, Wendy. *The Colors of Rhetoric.* Chicago: University of Chicago Press, 1982.

Stewart, Ann Harleman. "Kenning and Riddle in Old English." *Papers on Language and Literature* 15 (1979): 115–36.

Strauss, Barrie Ruth. "Women's Words as Weapons: Speech as Action in 'The Wife's Lament,' " *Texas Studies in Literature and Language* vol. 23 (Summer 1981): 268–85.

Tolkien, J. R. R. "*Beowulf*: The Monsters and the Critics," *An Anthology of*

Beowulf Criticism. Ed. Lewis E. Nicholson. Notre Dame: University of Notre Dame Press, 1971, 51–103.

Tompkins, Jane P., ed. *Reader-Response Criticism.* Baltimore: Johns Hopkins University Press, 1980.

Traugott, Elizabeth Closs. *A History of English Syntax.* New York: Holt, Rinehart and Winston, 1972.

Travis, Peter W. "Affective Criticism, the Pilgrimage of Reading, and Medieval English Literature," *Medieval Texts and Contemporary Readers.* Ed. Laurie A. Finke and Martin B. Schichtman. Ithaca: Cornell University Press, 1987, 201–15.

Vance, Eugene. *Mervelous Signals: Poetics and Sign Theory in the Middle Ages.* Lincoln: University of Nebraska Press, 1986.

Veblen, Thorstein. *Theory of the Leisure Class.* London: Macmillan, 1899.

Viswanathan, S. "On the Melting of the Sword: *Waelrapas* and the Engraving on the Sword-Hilt in *Beowulf*," *Philological Quarterly* 58 (1979): 360–63.

Wrenn, C. L., ed. *Beowulf with the Finnesburg Fragment.* London: Harrap, 1958.

Wyld, H. C. "Diction and Imagery in Anglo-Saxon Poetry," *Essays and Studies* 2 (1925): 49–91.

Zumthor, Paul. *Speaking of the Middle Ages.* Tr. Sarah White. Lincoln: University of Nebraska Press, 1986.

Index

Gillian R. Overing is Associate Professor of English at Wake Forest University, where she teaches Old English, linguistics, women's studies, and composition. In addition to articles on Old English literature and linguistic theory, she has published research on feminist pedagogy and writing theory, and has co-edited (with Cynthia L. Caywood) an anthology of essays, *Teaching Writing: Pedagogy, Gender and Equity* (SUNY Press, 1987). Her current research seeks to develop the dialogue between the traditional methodologies of Old English scholarship and contemporary feminist and semiotic theory.